M000222064

The Cybersecurity to English Dictionary

4th Edition

Raef Meeuwisse

Cyber Simplicity Ltd, 27 Old Gloucester Street, London, UK WC1N 3AX.

Email:	www.cybersimplicity.com (contact us)
Twitter:	@RaefMeeuwisse
First Edition*:	February 2016
Fourth Edition:	24 September 2018
Published by:	Cyber Simplicity Ltd

www.cybersimplicity.com

www.cybersecuritytoenglish.com

* note that an early version of this publication existed in *Cybersecurity for Beginners* prior to the first edition date.

Ordering Information:

Special discounts are available on quantity purchases by corporations, associations, educators, and others. For details, contact the publisher at the above listed address.

Trade and wholesalers: Please contact Cyber Simplicity Ltd.

Tel/Fax: +44(0)1227 540 540

ISBN-13:	978-1-911452-24-9 (paperback)
ISBN-13:	978-1-911452-26-3 (hardcover)
ISBN-13:	978-1-911452-25-6 (e-book)

DEDICATION

My thanks to all the readers of *Cybersecurity for Beginners*
for their ongoing feedback and additional suggestions
for cybersecurity-related terms. Keep them coming
via Twitter: #cybersecurityforbeginners
@RaefMeeuwisse

Risk does not respect bureaucracy.

Also Available

Also available from this author in paperback & digital formats:

Cybersecurity for Beginners
This book provides an easy insight into the full discipline of cybersecurity, even if you have a non-technical background.

Cybersecurity Exposed: The Cyber House Rules
Explores the causes for the increased magnitude and frequency of cybercrime. Why is cybersecurity frequently left vulnerable to attack? Is there a set of principles that can be applied to help correct these problems?

The Encrypted Pocketbook of Passwords
Writing down your passwords is usually fraught with risks. The Encrypted Pocketbook of Passwords helps you store your passwords more securely in a format that you can read but that others will find hard to break.

How to Hack a Human; Cybersecurity for the Mind
An overview of the social engineering, subliminal and conscious persuasion, digital reconnaissance and psychographic techniques designed to control and influence human behavior.

Cybersecurity: Home and Small Business
Guidance on the basic security practices we can apply at home or in small businesses to help decrease the risk of being successfully attacked.

Visit www.cybersimplicity.com for a full list of the latest titles.

Looking for great corporate promotional gifts?
Check out our offers at www.cybersimplicity.com

Raef Meeuwisse

CONTENTS

Disclaimer:

The language of cybersecurity is constantly evolving and terms may be open to different interpretation by different sources. This text is designed to provide basic, initial guidance only and no warranty is implied or provided.

INTRODUCTION

Have you ever been to one of those meetings where they throw out a new term and you need to find out what it means as soon as possible? The field of cybersecurity is stacked full of new words and phrases. Without easy access to a set of cybersecurity definitions, life can be difficult.

This dictionary will help you stay on top of all the main terms that cybersecurity professionals use. You may even find some words you can throw into the mix to impress your colleagues.

And, you will finally be able to translate what a cybersecurity professional says into plain English:

*'We got **doxxed** and **pwned** by a **hacktivist** through a **RAT takedown.**'*

Becomes:

'We got our **personal information revealed** in a **humiliating attack** by a **rogue individual trying to prove a political point** using a **remote access tool** to create **widespread intrusion and disruption** to our organization.'

This dictionary began life as a glossary of definitions at the back of my book *Cybersecurity for Beginners*.

As I wrote that book, it became apparent that there was no easy-to-read repository of information to help people understand all the main terms used in the field of cybersecurity. Due to space and size limitations, I could not include all the terms in that book, so I set about creating a specific, expanded dictionary as a separate (and cheaper) publication.

My aim with this dictionary is to provide easy, fast access to straightforward definitions of the most frequently encountered terms that crop up in many facets of cybersecurity.

However, the field of cybersecurity is quickly evolving. *Fileless malware*, *cryptojacking*, *quantum cryptography* and updates to the OWASP top 10 threat titles are among the terms added in this edition. In fact, this fourth edition is over 30% larger than the third edition.

As there are so many pieces of malware now in existence, I have not clogged the book with hundreds of names for known, specific malware threats, though I have included a very small number of the most infamous common vulnerabilities and exposures (CVEs).

Please note that in cases in which a term has more than one form – for example, when it exists as both an acronym and a short set of words – the definition has been placed against the most frequently used version. For example, the term *OWASP* is usually used to refer to the **O**pen **W**eb **A**pplication **S**ecurity **P**roject, so the definition is located against the acronym because that is the most frequently used form of this term. There is also an entry for the ***Open Web Application Security Project*** that directs the reader to refer to the *OWASP* entry to view the definition.

If a term is more frequently used in its fuller form, the acronym will still be present, but will refer the reader to the more commonly used form to view the definition.

If you have any additional terms that you would like me to define or if you think any existing definitions should be clarified, please feel free to tweet me on **@RaefMeeuwisse** and I will aim to add the best suggestions to future versions of this dictionary.

If you are interested in learning about the basics of cybersecurity, I recommend my book *Cybersecurity for Beginners*.

The Cybersecurity to English Dictionary

Fourth Edition

Cyber Attack Basics:

Hostile parties (**threat actors**)
seek
vulnerabilities (security gaps)
to
exploit (take advantage of)
for
financial or political gain.

THE CYBERSECURITY TO ENGLISH DICTIONARY

(Bolded text in these definitions refers to terms defined in the dictionary)

A is for Advanced Persistent Threats

acceptable use policy – a set of wording that describes an agreement between any user and the enterprise that owns the service, **application** or **device** being accessed. The agreement usually defines both the primary permitted and prohibited activities.

Access Control List (ACL) – a record (list) of the people, **devices**, **application** services and other accounts that have been allowed or denied permission to enter a particular location. The location may be as small as a single file, or as large as an enterprise **network**. The permission can usually be refined so the rights to view, create, modify, delete or administer can be individually selected or de-selected. To streamline the process of granting permissions, **access groups** with values such as 'All Employees' and 'All Managers' are often used. Permissions are usually defined at a parent level (for example across a device or folder) and items within that same folder or device hierarchy will usually be set to inherit the permissions from the parent.

access controls – rules and techniques used to manage and restrict entry to or exit from a physical, virtual or digital area through the use of permissions. Permissions are usually assigned individually to a person, **device** or **application** service to ensure **accountability** and traceability of usage. The permissions can be secured using (i) physical tokens (something you have); for example a **key** card (ii) secret information (something you know); such as a **password** or (iii) **biometric** information – using part of the human body such as a fingerprint or eye scan to gain access (something you are). See also **multi-factor authentication**.

access group – a pre-defined list of user accounts that share a common set of permission requirements, such as 'All Employees.' The process of using access groups allows for more efficient administration, as, for example, the 'All Employees' group can be administered in one place but referred to in multiple **access control lists**.

access rights – the set of permissions granted to a user account to define whether that account can enter and use specific functions within a **network**, **application**, **system** or hardware **device**. Usually these permissions are granted on the basis of **least privilege**. See also **least privilege**.

accountability – the security principle of ensuring that all critical **assets** and actions have clear ownership and traceability to identify who is responsible for them. See also **single point accountability**.

ACL – acronym for **Access Control List**.

active defense – the use of digital bait and traps such as a **honeypot** or **sinkhole** to detect, deter or trap **attacker**s.

active memory – see **in-memory**.

adaptive access – a technology that can increase or decrease the strength and number of **authentication** checks depending on the level of prevailing **risk**. For example, such a technology is usually context aware and can increase the authentication checks whenever an active **threat** is known to be operating. The same technology can choose to decrease the authentication checks required from an internal resource working onsite on low-risk **data** at his or her regular location during his or her normal working day.

Adaptive Content Inspection (ACI) – see **deep content inspection**.

adaptive defense – the use of agile techniques to rapidly learn and adjust **cyber** protection **method**s to help decrease the possibility of successful **attack** or to reduce the window of time between detection and **incident** counter-response. See also **Indicators of Compromise (IOC)**.

admin access – see **administrative access**.

administrative access – any electronic account that has the authority to perform elevated activities. An elevated activity is any action that can apply significant changes to one or more **digital devices**, software **applications** or services. For example, the permission to install new software, or to permit additional user access are considered elevated privileges requiring this elevated **authorization** level. This term is often abbreviated to 'admin access.'

administrative permission – the process of granting authority to an account belonging to a person, group or computing process so that the account can perform elevated access actions associated with **administrative access**. See **administrative access**.

administrator – a person or **system** with an account that provides them with privileged **administrative access**.

Advanced Encryption Standard (AES) – this is a symmetrical **method** of **cipher**ing information from plain characters to and from secret, encoded information. Symmetrical means that the same **key** that is used to cipher the information is used to decipher the information. This standard was originally introduced as a successor to the **Data Encryption Standard (DES)** and **Triple DES**. See also **encryption** and **symmetrical encryption**.

Advanced Persistent Threats (APTs) – a term used to describe the tenacious and highly evolved set of tactics used by **hackers** to infiltrate **networks** through **digital devices** and to then leave malicious software in place for as long as possible. The **cyber attack lifecycle** usually involves the **attacker** performing research & reconnaissance, preparing the most effective **attack** tools, getting an initial foothold into the network or the target **digital landscape**, spreading the infection and adjusting the range of attack tools in place to then **exploit** the position to maximum advantage. The purpose can be to steal or **corrupt** an organization's digital **data** or to extort money from the organization and/or disrupt its operations, for either financial gain, brand damage or other political purposes. This form of sophisticated attack becomes harder and more costly to resolve the further into the lifecycle the attackers are and the longer they have managed to already leave the malicious software in place. A goal with this **threat** type is for the intruder to remain (persist) undetected for as long as possible in order to maximize the opportunities presented by the intrusion – for example, to steal **data** over a long period of time. See also **kill-chain**.

Advanced Threat Defense (ATD) – this term describes the ways in which very large organizations use a wider range of protective techniques to detect, deny, disrupt, degrade, deceive and contain any unauthorized attempts at entry into a **digital landscape**. For example, an organization's Advanced Threat Defense may include extending protection beyond **anti-malware**, **encryption** and **firewalls** to include the use of coordinated **network traffic analysis**, **payload analysis**,

network forensics, **endpoint behavior analysis** and **endpoint forensics**, often also using **artificial intelligence** to more actively analyze, identify and respond to emerging **threats** and **attacks**.

adware – any computer program (software) designed to render adverts to an end user. This type of software can be considered a form of **malware** if (i) the advertising was not **consent**ed to by the user, (ii) it is made difficult to uninstall or remove, or (iii) it provides other covert malware functions.

AES – see **Advanced Encryption Standard**.

agile – a term used as a prefix to indicate that a process or methodology takes a flexible approach to the realization of requirements. For example, within a standard process, requirements are usually fixed, but time and/or resources may be adjusted to allow the requirements to be met. Within an agile process, time and/or resources may be fixed but the requirements are prioritized and adjusted to meet the fixed time and or resource constraints. This can be used to help guarantee regular delivery, for example, by using a fixed delivery time but adjusting which requirements will be met in the time allowed.

AI – see **artificial intelligence**.

AI anti-malware – security software designed to defeat malicious software (**malware**) by understanding and learning its patterns of behavior. Unlike security software that works based on **signatures**, where the program has to know what the **threat** looks like to block it, security software based on **artificial intelligence** (**AI**) can identify most threats even when it has not encountered them on any prior occasion. Due to the rise of **single-use malware** and the tens of millions of unique new malware threats discovered each month, this technology has become essential for the protection of most **digital devices**.

AI-driven threat intelligence – the use of **artificial intelligence** to analyze, filter and determine the most significant potential sources of **attack** or **vulnerability** for a particular **digital landscape**. Due to the vast complexity and number of potential **risk**s to each environment, this technology can help process and report much larger volumes of information than would be possible from using only manual processes.

air gap – the use of some form of physical and electronic separation to ensure that activities in one area cannot impact or infect activities in another. Used in the context of **cybersecurity** to describe a security measure in which sensitive or infected **systems** are physically and digitally isolated so they have no possibility of interacting with any other systems and **networks**.

alert status – an escalation flag that can be assigned to a **security incident** to indicate that it cannot be managed inside allowable time limits or other acceptable tolerances that are defined by an organization's security processes.

all source intelligence – a term defined by the US **National Initiative for Cybersecurity Education** (**NICE**) to refer to gathering together **threat intelligence** and information from all appropriate internal and external sources for the purpose of gaining insight into and understanding the implications of new and active potential **threats**.

altcoin – any **cryptocurrency** that is not **Bitcoin**. "Alternative cryptocurrency to Bit**coin**."

anti-malware – is a computer program designed to look for specific files and behaviors (**signatures**) that indicate the presence or the attempted installation of malicious software. If or when detected, the program seeks to isolate the **attack** (**quarantine** or block the **malware**), remove it, if it can, and also alert appropriate people to the attempt or to the presence of the malware. The program can be **host-based** (installed on **devices**

that are directly used by people) or **network-based** (installed on **gateway** devices through which information is passed). Older forms of this software could detect only specific, pre-defined forms of malicious software using signature files. Newer forms use **machine learning** and make use of additional techniques including **behavior monitoring**. See also **malware**.

anti-spyware – a subset of **anti-malware** software that has the specific purpose of detecting, blocking or preventing the installation or operation of malicious software used to illicitly monitor user behavior, improve ad targeting and sometimes steal information. See also **spyware**.

anti-virus – predecessor of **anti-malware** software that was used before the nature and types of malicious software had diversified. This is a computer program designed to look for the presence or installation of specific files. If or when detected, the program seeks to isolate the **attack** (**quarantine** or block the **virus**), remove it, if it can, and also alert appropriate people to the attempt. A virus is only one form of **malware**, so the term anti-malware is considered to be more inclusive of other forms of malicious software. However, as people are more familiar with the term 'anti-virus,' this can sometimes be used to describe various types of anti-malware. See also **anti-malware** and **virus**.

application – a collection of functions and instructions in electronic format (a **software program**) that resides across one or more **digital devices**, usually designed to create, modify, process, store, inspect and/or transmit specific types of **data**. For subversive applications, see **malware**.

APT – see **Advanced Persistent Threat**.

artificial intelligence – the development of knowledge and skills in computer programs (**applications**) to the extent that they are able to perform perception, recognition, translation and/or decision-making activities without prior direct experience of the event. **Machine learning** is a less advanced form of artificial intelligence where the functionality is more focused. See also **singularity**, **digital sentience** and **synthetic intelligence**.

assessments – the evaluation of a target (for example an **application**, service, or supplier) against specific goals, objectives or other criteria through the collection of information about it. Usually, this is achieved through an established and repeatable process that involves discussing or answering questions about the target's capabilities and approaches. The purpose is to understand how closely the target meets the intended criteria and to identify any gaps or deficiencies. An assessment is different than an **audit** because it does not necessarily check for evidence (proof) that the responses are genuine and does not need to be carried out by an objective third party. It can be considered that a security assessment is usually akin to a consultative audit that does not seek to catch out or disprove the evidence provided by the target being examined.

asset – any item (physical or digital) that has inherent value. For **cybersecurity**, information items that can be monetized (for example, intellectual property and sets of personal **data**) are regarded as high-value assets due to their potential resale or blackmail value.

asymmetric backdoor – a covert entry and/or exit point that uses cryptographic **key**s set by an **attacker**, so that only this attacker can use the **backdoor**, even after it is discovered. See also **kleptography**.

asymmetric cryptography – a **method** of **cipher**ing information using two different **key**s (a **key pair**). One is a **public key**, the other is a **private key**. One key is used to cipher the information from plain text into a secret format. The other key can then be used to decipher the secret format back to plain text. The keys can be used in any order as long as both keys are used. As one key is public, the use of the private key first is usually only for the purpose of attaching a **digital signature**. A single key cannot be used to cipher and decipher the same message (single key use to cipher and decipher information is called **symmetric cryptography**). Also known as **public key encryption** and **public key cryptography**.

ATD – see **Advanced Threat Defense**.

attack – the occurrence of an unauthorized intrusion.

attack and penetration test – see **penetration testing**.

attacker – an umbrella term used to cover all types of people and organizations that may attempt to gain **unauthorized access** to a **digital device, application, system** or **network**. See also **black hat, hacker, hacktivist, cyber warrior, script kiddies**… as examples of **cyber attacker**s on the ever-growing list of specific attacker types.

attack lifecycle – see **cyber attack lifecycle**.

attack mechanism – a term that describes the **method** used to achieve an unauthorized intrusion.

attack method – the technique, tools or **exploit** used by an adversary to attempt to gain **unauthorized access** to any part of a **digital landscape**.

attack signature – a distinctive pattern of characteristics that can be identified to help understand and correct an attempt at **unauthorized access** or intrusion. See also **indicators of compromise (IOC)**.

attack surface – the sum of the potential exposure area that could be used to gain unauthorized entry to any part of a **digital landscape**. This area usually includes perimeter **network** hardware (such as **firewalls**) and **web servers** (hardware that hosts Internet-enabled **applications**). It can also include extended areas of the landscape such as external applications, supplier services and mobile **devices** that have permission to access information or services of value. See also **cyber defense points**.

attack vector – a path or means that could be used by an unauthorized party to gain access to a **digital device**, **network** or **system**.

attacker dwell time – see **dwell time**.

attribution – the identification of the perpetrator (**threat actor**) behind a specific **cyber attack**. This is usually achieved by uncovering evidence through the use of **digital forensic** techniques. The majority of **attacker**s use tactics that intentionally include false or misleading digital clues (**cyber false flags**), so the reliability of any subsequent identification by digital techniques alone is easier to challenge and discredit.

audits – the use of one or more independent examiners (auditors) to check if a target product, service and/or location is meeting the specific required **control** standards. This form of inspection requires that individual controls are tested to confirm their suitability and consistent usage. The outcomes from this type of event, including any gaps discovered and corrective actions required, are always provided in a final report.

augmented reality – the overlaying of a virtual digital layer of information onto a view of the real world. The digital layer may seem to interact with the real world, but the impact is limited to affecting the perspective of the user (or users) who are immersed in the experience. This differs from **virtual reality**, in which the immersed users can only perceive a fully artificial world. Advanced versions of augmented reality can map and understand objects and surfaces, and can then seem to allow digital projections to interact with real-world objects. See also

metaverse and **mixed reality**.

authentication – the process of confirming whether the identity and other properties of any entity (person or **application**) are valid and genuine. See also **multi-factor authentication**.

authorization – the use of **authentication** information together with **access control list**s to verify whether or not an entity (person or **application**) has permission to perform the function it is requesting.

availability – the assignment of a value to a set of information to indicate how much disruption or outage the owner considers to be acceptable. Often this is expressed or translated into a scale of time. **Data** with the highest possible availability rating would be required to be readily accessible at all times (no downtime permitted), often through the use of a fully redundant failsafe. The value assigned to the information's availability is used by the owner of an **application** or service to set the **recovery time objective**. See also **integrity** – a different, but related term.

B is for Botnet

backdoor – a covert **method** of accessing software or a **device** that bypasses the normal **authentication** requirements.

backup – (i) the process of archiving a copy of something so that it can be restored following a disruption. (ii) having a redundant (secondary) capability to continue a process, service or **application** if the primary capability is disrupted.

baiting – the act of an **attacker** offering an item of perceived value, usually for free, in an area where potential victims may notice and acquire it. The item of value is either poisoned in some way (for example, it may contain unwelcome and unforeseen content, such as malicious software) or is used as a method for identifying and establishing contact and commitment with a potential victim to influence, persuade or coerce them into a more significant scam or attack. If the item is not offered for free but in return for something from the user, then the attack type can be considered a **quidproquo** rather than baiting. An example of baiting can be to offer or leave free USB storage device that is pre-loaded with **malware**.

bashdoor – alternative name for the family of security **bugs** also known as **shellshock**. See entry for **shellshock**.

BCP – see **Business Continuity Plan**.

BeEF – see **Browser Exploitation Framework**.

BeEF hook – the process of getting a user to visit a vulnerable web **application** that can be **exploited** to **inject** unauthorized instructions (code) into his or her web-browsing software. Once the code is injected, the browser is registered (hooked) to a server (the BeEF server), and is able to respond to commands from it to perform actions that are unwanted, unauthorized and potentially unknown to the owner or user. See also **Browser Exploitation Framework**.

behavioral detection – the identification of actions or activity patterns displayed by a person, computer program or hardware component that seem to be atypical or irregular. This identification is usually performed by software based on rules set up by a security specialist. Once identified, any irregular patterns can trigger alerts and investigation into the possibility that these abnormal activities indicate an impending or ongoing **attack** or other compromise. As an example, geo-behavioral detection identifies when the user credentials are used from an impossible location (logging on from a different continent within minutes of logging in from a home continent).

behavioral microtargeting – the capability to influence or persuade people based on a precise understanding of their behaviors and personality preferences. This level of individual categorization and understanding is widespread due to the use of **cookies** and 'free' services that have monetized their offerings through the sale of advertising. See also **psychographics**.

behavior monitoring – a **method** of surveillance to check for actions or activities that may indicate rogue or undesirable intent.

BGP – see **Border Gateway Protocol**.

biometrics – the use of physical qualities and attributes as a form of identity **authentication**. Fingerprint scans, retina scans and facial recognition are all examples of biometrics. As fast as new biometric options are created, the means to defeat them often follow. For this reason, biometrics is usually used only as part of a **multi-factor authentication**.

Bitcoin – a decentralized, virtual digital currency (**cryptocurrency**) and payment **system**, based on a distributed, public ledger. The currency provides a high degree of transactional anonymity as balances and ledger entries are associated with private cryptographic **key**s and not with the individual or company that uses the system (lose your key, lose your money). This has made it, along with other digital currencies, a payment **method** of choice for **cyber criminals**, who also use it to receive **cyber** blackmail payments. The invention of Bitcoin is also associated with the invention of a sophisticated **encryption**-based authenticity technique known as **blockchain**. See also **blockchain**.

black-box penetration testing – is the term used to describe a situation in which no advance information about the technical details of a computer program has been made available to those who are checking it for **vulnerabilities**. Whomever is performing the **penetration testing** is operating without any inside knowledge, so the term is used to indicate a lack of visibility inside the 'box' (program) that is being checked.

black hat – a person who engages in attempts to gain **unauthorized access** to one or more **digital devices** with nefarious (criminal or unethical) objectives. A **hacker** with unethical goals, or no perceived ethical goals.

black-listing – (in the context of **cybersecurity**) means adding a specific file type, **URL** or **data packet** to a security defense program to prevent it from being directly accessed or used. For example, a website **domain** can be blocked using **firewall** rules to ensure that no user can visit that website through customary means.

black swan – an event that comes as a surprise, has a major impact and after analysis is falsely rationalized as predictable after the event. Some security analysts assert that certain **cyber megabreaches** are black swan events; however, the gaps identified during root cause analysis of any megabreach always turn out to result from at least 3 critical gaps in the standard security that should have been present. A legitimate black swan event would not include causes that demonstrate the absence of established security countermeasures. See also **stacked risk**.

bleeding edge – using inventions so new, they have the likelihood to cause damage to their population before they become stable and safe.

blended threat – the use of a combination of a number of different **malware** techniques and/or **attack method**s in a single attack to increase the impact and make the intrusion harder to defeat or eliminate. See also **polymorphic malware** and **metamorphic malware** as examples.

blockchain – a **method** developed as part of the **cryptocurrency** known as **Bitcoin** to **authenticate** valid transactions. A distributed, public ledger of transactions is created, with each new entry leveraging an **encrypted** hash value from the last entry in the ledger. This means that the ledger is stronger than previously-designed authenticity techniques. Theoretically, falsification of an entry would require not only the **encryption** to be broken or changed but also the full sequence of entries in all public copies of the ledger to be adjusted. This technique (and a private variation) is now expected to be widely adopted as a standard method for assuring authenticity across digital **platform**s where authenticity is required.

blue team – the group of people who assemble during a mock **attack** by a **red team** to help defend the **digital landscape** being targeted.

Bluetooth – a short-range wireless standard for the connection of **devices**.

bogus boss – a form of **social engineering** scam where a **cyber criminal** impersonates a person in a position of senior authority within a company as a means to extract information or payment. The contact from the fraudster may come through email, phone or another communication channel. This scam is also sometimes referred to as the CEO (Chief Executive Officer) scam.

Boolean – a **data** type with only 2 options, usually 1 or 0. This originated from a **method** of combining algebra with binary that became extensively used within computer programming and electronics for expressing logic. Typically the setting *1* is used for *true* and *0* for *false*. This was first explored by George Boole (1847) in a book called *The Mathematical Expression of Logic*. During the twentieth century, logic gates and Boolean algebra became pivotal to expressing logic within electronics and computer programming.

Border Gateway Protocol (BGP) – is a standard format that different **systems** on a **network** can use to share and make decisions about the path (routing) for information being transmitted.

borked – a term to describe when something ceases to work correctly due to some error or negligence by the organization or person responsible for it.

bot – is a computer program designed to perform specific tasks. They are usually simple, small and designed to perform fast, repetitive tasks. When the purpose of the program conflicts with an organization's goals and needs, for example, where the bot is designed to remotely execute the instructions of an attacker, a bot can be considered to be a form of **malware**. See also **botnet**.

bot herder – is a **hacker** who uses automated techniques to seek vulnerable **networks** and **systems**. The bot herder's initial goal is to install or find **bot** programs that can be used to achieve a particular purpose. Once one or more bots are in place, the hacker can **control** these programs to perform a larger objective of stealing, **corrupt**ing and/or disrupting information, **assets** and services. See also **botnet, command and control server** and **Mirai** (an example of a botnet).

bot master – alternative naming convention for a **bot herder**. This term also signifies that the person referred to has operational authority over the **command and control servers** or other programs used to instruct a **botnet**.

botnet – shortened version of ro**bot**ic **net**work. A connected set of programs designed to operate together over a **network** (including the **Internet**) to achieve specific purposes. These purposes can be good or bad. Some programs of this type are used to help support Internet connections, while malicious uses include taking **control** of some or all of a computer's functions to support large-scale service **attacks** (see **denial of service**).

Original designs of botnets used **command and control servers** as intermediaries to help deliver instructions. Recent versions of this attack type can now be designed to communicate with only a **peer-to-peer** connection, making it harder to combat them through the defense technique known as **decapitation**. A botnet is sometimes referred to as a **zombie army**.

breach notification procedure – some types of information, when suspected or known to be lost or stolen, must, by law, be reported to one or more authorities within a defined time period. Usually, this type of regulation applies to personal information. The required notification time period varies, but is often within 24 hours after the known or suspected breach takes place. In addition to reporting the known or suspected loss to the authorities, the lead organization responsible for the information (referred to as the **data controller**) is also required to swiftly notify anyone who is affected, and later on, must submit (to appropriate regulators) a full root cause analysis and information about how the organization responded and fixed any issues that were identified. To meet these legal obligations, larger companies usually have a pre-defined breach notification procedure to ensure that the timelines are met. The fines for data breaches are usually increased or decreased based on the adequacy of the organization's breach and **incident response** management.

brick – in the context of **cybersecurity**, this term can be used to describe when an attack on a **digital device** has rendered it so useless, it can be considered as useful as a building block (brick). *To brick a device* is effectively to render it inoperative.

broken access control – OWASP lists this as one of the top 10 critical security flaws that should be guarded against. This flaw involves a situation in which a user who has authorized and valid access (**authentication**) has not been correctly confirmed, or in which the confirmed connection between the **authenticate**d user and a web-based **application** (the **session management**) is hijacked, lost, transferred or otherwise **corrupt**ed.

broken authentication and session management – previously listed as an **OWASP** top 10 critical security flaw. This term was replaced by **broken access control** and has the same meaning. See **broken access control** (above).

Browser Exploitation Framework – also known as **BeEF**, is a toolset designed to help perform **cyber attacks** or **penetration testing** by taking advantage of **vulnerabilities** in the software that people use to interact with the Internet (their **web browser**/s). Traffic to and from any web browser bypasses many of the security layers typically in place for Internet use and can potentially be used to create beachheads inside otherwise secure perimeters. Once an **attacker** is inside, he or she can launch further attempts to **exploit** and **corrupt** an environment. See also **BeEF hook**.

brute force (attack) – the use of a systematic approach that can quickly generate large volumes of possible **methods** to gain **unauthorized access** to a computer **system**. For example, an automated **script** can run through the large but finite number of possibilities to try to guess a given eight-character **password** in a matter of seconds. Computing speeds make brute force attempts to try millions of possibilities easy if other defenses are not present. A common defense against this type of **attack** is to detect and block more than a few attempts at guessing any security information.

buffer overflow – exceeding the allocated capacity of the electronic **memory** used to temporarily store **data** when it is being moved between locations. This process is used by some forms of **malware** to **exploit** an electronic target.

bug – a flaw or fault in an **application** or **system**. The term originated from very early computers that had huge capacitors that could become defective if physical insects (bugs) were present and shorted the connection.

bug bounty – a finder's fee that some companies offer to people who are the first to find and report a security **vulnerability** in their software or service. This acts as a monetary incentive for skilled, but ethical, **hackers** to identify and report potential security gaps so the organization that owns the **platform** can address the issue before anyone else finds and exposes the problem. See also **bug poacher** (below).

bug poacher – a person who performs the uninvited detection of a security gap or issue in software or in another digital service (**platform**) for the purpose of selling information about the problem to the owner. The term 'poacher' is used to reflect the uninvited nature of the action; usually companies or organizations that do not offer a **bug bounty** program are the ones that use this term.

Business Continuity Plan (abbreviation **BCP**) – an operational document that describes how an organization can restore its critical products or services to its customers, should a substantial event that causes disruption to normal operations occur. An effective business continuity plan will link to multiple **technical disaster recovery plan**s that describe in more detail how each dependent product or service can be technically restored.

BYOC – acronym for **B**ring **Y**our **O**wn **C**loud. A term used to describe the **cybersecurity** status in which employees or contractors are making direct decisions to use externally hosted services to manage at least some of their organization's work. If this is taking place without the inclusion of a process to **risk** assess and **control** the security features, it can lead to significant risks both to the direct information involved and to the rest of the **digital landscape** by potentially opening up other security gaps.

BYOD – acronym for **B**ring **Y**our **O**wn **D**evice, indicating that employees and other authorized people are allowed to bring some of their own **digital devices** into the workplace to use for some work purposes. Some security people also use this term for 'Bring Your Own Disaster' due to the uncontrollable number of security variables that this practice introduces for any information allowed to flow onto or through personal devices.

C is for Cloud

C&C server – see **command and control server**.

cache – a location where computers store information they anticipate may soon be needed for processing, in order to accelerate performance. Information is sometimes retained in this location slightly before and after usage, making it a frequent target for **malware**, especially as information in the cache usually needs to be held in plain text (un**encrypted**) for processing.

CAPA – acronym meaning **c**orrective **a**ction **p**reventive **a**ction. See also **corrective and preventive action system**.

carding – the acquisition or sale of stolen credit card details by people, websites or organizations.

CASB – see **Cloud Access Security Broker**.

CEO scam – see **bogus boss**.

CERT – acronym used widely to mean either **C**omputer **E**mergency **R**esponse **T**eam (for example CERT UK) or **C**omputer **E**mergency **R**eadiness **T**eam (for example CERT US). See also **US CERT**. The primary role of these organizations is to help their member or country organizations to prepare for, monitor and respond to **cybersecurity** and other **digital landscape threats**.

certificate authority – the use of a trusted third party organization to supply and verify tokens (certificates) that attest to the validity of a technology service.

chain of custody – a **method** of ensuring that a set of information and any metadata (tags, labels or other descriptive additions) are preserved as they are passed between owners and locations. This term is frequently applied to the preservation of evidence in the field of **digital forensics**.

chargeware – a form of malicious software (**malware**) designed to perform actions on a victim's **device** that will incur costs to the victim for the benefit of the **attacker**. For example, on a **smart** mobile phone, sending **SMS** text messages out to a premium rate number without the owner's knowledge or **consent**.

checksum – a **method** of using a mathematical algorithm to verify that any collection of information is still exactly as it was. If any piece of information in the collection has changed, the value that results from running the algorithm will be changed, indicating that the information has been altered. See also **md5 hash** as an example.

Chief Information Security Officer (**CISO**) – an individual who functions as the single point of accountability in any organization for ensuring that an appropriate framework for managing dangers and **threats** to electronic and physical information **assets** is operating and effective.

CI – see **continuous integration**.

cipher – the use of a **key** to change information into a secret or hidden format.

CISO – see **Chief Information Security Officer**.

clear-box penetration testing – see **white-box penetration testing**.

CLI – see **command line interface**.

clickbait – enticing content generated by advertisers or criminals that encourages or pressures the recipient, or viewer, to want to access the **URL** link or attached file that is on offer. Originally this term was used to describe **method**s that advertisers would use to drive traffic to a particular webpage; however, it is also a primary technique used to make **phishing** communications attractive to the unwary recipient.

clopen – a **network** or **system** that is intended to be run as closed and secure, but due to size, scale, **threats** or security deficiencies, is constantly identifying and seeking to eliminate new intrusions. A portmanteau of the words **clo**sed and **open**.

closed system – a collection of **applications**, **systems** and **devices** that only have the ability to communicate with each other. No connection to any component outside the known and trusted group is permitted.

Cloud Access Security Broker (**CASB**) – is a service that can be used to help an organization more efficiently deploy and maintain improved **cyber** protection measures on services that are provided by external suppliers (**cloud** providers). This type of service can be used to enforce standards such as specific **encryption** and **authentication** requirements to improve **resilience** and decrease the **risk** of compromise from a single point of **control**. This can be used to help reinforce the standards of a **security architecture**.

cloud computing – the use of remote servers hosted on the Internet. The term '**cloud**' refers to the user's lack of knowledge about exactly where the processing or actions they are performing are being handled. Often a cloud symbol is used to denote the lack of specific information being made available in a representation. A **public cloud** is a low-cost, multi-tenant environment in which resources are rapidly shared and re-provisioned across many different customers using virtualization technology (see **virtual machine**). It is also possible to have a **private cloud** not hosted on the Internet. When that occurs, the term *cloud* is still used to denote a lack of transparency about the exact physical machines on which the computing is occurring. However, a private cloud can also be hosted over the Internet using security measures designed to keep the resources exclusive to the customer.

cloudlet – a very small **data center** designed to help **cloud** facilities improve their proximity to **devices** that require faster response times (lower latency). For example, within **fog computing**, instead of a single, remote and very large data center providing **cloud computing**, a number of distributed cloudlets can help to provide faster, more distributed and more resilient computational power.

cloud security – a term used to describe the collective **policies**, technologies, **procedures** and other **controls** that are used to protect a technology service hosted by an external organization. **Cloud platform**s are typically Internet accessible and shared with many customers, requiring stronger security than services delivered within an isolated **network** require.

cloud (**the**) – an umbrella term used to identify any technology service that uses software and equipment not physically managed or owned by the person or organization (customer) using it. This usually provides the advantage of on-demand scalability at lower cost. Examples include **applications** that are hosted online, online file storage areas, and even remote virtual computers. Using a cloud means the equipment managing the service is run by the cloud provider and not by the customer. But although the customer does not own the service, he or she is still accountable for the information that he or she chooses to store and process through it. Usually a cloud service is identified by an 'aaS' suffix. For example – **SaaS** (Software as a Service), **IaaS** (Infrastructure as a Service) and **PaaS** (Platform as a Service).

COBIT – acronym for **C**ontrol **Ob**jectives for **I**nformation **T**echnology, a security, **governance** and management framework for enterprise information technologies developed by **ISACA**.

command and control servers – one or more centralized computer programs used to communicate instructions to and / or information from a **botnet**. Also known as a **C&C server**.

Command Line Interface (CLI) – a **method** of interacting directly with the heart of a computer **system** (for example, its **operating system**) so that it can receive and respond to instructions.

compartmentalization – a security technique that can be applied to high-value **assets**. The assets can be placed in a more isolated **system**, **network** or **device** requiring additional security **controls** to access. This is designed to add greater protection for those assets. When this is done within a device, it may also be a form of **containerization**. **Network segmentation** is also a form of compartmentalization.

compliance – the process used to verify that **governance** items (**policies, procedures**, regulations and more) are being followed, and to identify when they are not. **Audits, assessments**, and **continuous monitoring** can be used to identify and report compliance deficiencies. Any identified gaps are usually tracked and resolved through a **corrective and preventive action system**.

Computer Emergency Response Team – see **CERT**.

computer virus – see **virus**.

confidentiality – the assignment of a value to a set of information to indicate the level of secrecy and the access restrictions required to prevent unauthorized people from viewing it. A typical example of a confidentiality scale is: (i) Public Use (ii) Internal Use (iii) Confidential (iv) Strictly Confidential and (v) Restricted.

configuration management – the backbone of security management in large enterprises, this is the process used to track and ensure that all hardware and software are identified and are kept in a controlled state. Functions include (i) helping to ensure that timely security **patch management** can be applied and that (ii) unknown **digital devices** can be prevented from connecting to the **network**.

consent – when electronic personal information is involved, there are often legal constraints that govern how the **data** can be used and where the information can be viewed, stored, transmitted or otherwise processed. In these circumstances, permission is often required from each individual to specify what information can be collected, where it can be processed and for how long it will be retained. These permissions can be represented by a series of tags on individual records or on the full data set. The attributes that require explicit permission may include, but are not limited to, country of origin, permission for export, limitations of use, retention and notification requirements.

containerization – (i) the partitioning of software functions within a single **device, system** or **network** that is sufficient to isolate it from potential harm or from other unwanted interactions with other software in the same environment or device. (ii) the complete isolation of one technology from another. For networks, this is also referred to as **network segmentation**. See also **zero trust**.

containment – a stage during an **incident response** when steps are taken to isolate a confirmed problem (for example a **malware** infection) to prevent the issue from spreading to other areas.

content filtering – see **packet filtering**.

content inspection – a security **procedure** that can be performed by some security technologies to analyze electronic information, either when the information is at rest or more often, when the information is in transit. The degree to which the content can be inspected may depend on whether the **data** is **encrypt**ed and whether the security technology has access to the decryption **key**s.

content inspection and security gateways – a type of security product that combines **content inspection** capabilities (see above) with other security techniques such as advanced **firewall** protection. These are usually deployed at the perimeter of **network**s or network segments but in high value environments may also be placed on end user **digital devices** such as laptop computers and smartphones.

continuous integration – the process of repeatedly consolidating new software code with existing software code during the development or update stage to help verify and test for any emerging issues, errors or security gaps. Usually the process makes use of a centrally shared repository and automated tool to allow the work of several different developers to be continually converged. See also **DevSecOps**.

continuous monitoring – using technology to actively monitor the ongoing security of an **application**, website or other electronic service. The purpose is to provide faster alerts when any significant infringements of security that create potential **risks** are detected. For example, continuous automated monitoring for **port** scanning can detect patterns that may indicate an imminent **attack** and alert the appropriate personnel.

continuous network visibility – an attribute of hyper-secure environments in which an ongoing and real-time understanding of an organization's interconnected computing **devices** is maintained. The purpose is to aid in early identification and rectification of any issues.

control – (in the context of security and **compliance**) a **method** of regulating something, often a process, technology or behavior, to achieve a desired outcome, usually resulting in the reduction of **risk**. Depending on how it is designed and used, any single control may be referred to as preventive, detective or corrective.

control information – the component of a **data packet** that provides the destination, source and type of content.

control modes – an umbrella term for preventive, detective and corrective **method**s of defense. Each of these methods represents a different time posture. **Preventive controls** are designed to stop an **attack** <u>before</u> it is successful, **detective controls** are designed to monitor and raise an alert <u>during</u> a potential compromise and **corrective controls** are the rectification of an issue <u>after</u> an event.

control systems – collections of **applications** that function together to command the actions or activities of **devices**. For example, a heating, ventilation and air-conditioning (HVAC) control system may contain a number of devices (sensors) that feed into a central set of applications which regulate other devices (heaters and coolers). Collectively, this would be an example of a control system. **Industrial control systems** is a term applied when the usage is for large-scale production objectives and/or for operating extremely high-capacity devices. These **systems** are considered to be high-value targets for **cyber attack** because they are easy to ransom, expensive to repair, have substantial ability to disrupt or halt business operations and can lead to huge brand and share price damage.

cookie – (in the context of **cybersecurity**) – a very small piece of electronic information stored as a file on a user's computer when he or she accesses a web page. This file was originally intended to help users and websites remember information such as the contents of a shopping cart after a user has moved on to another web page or whether or not the user is an existing subscriber. However, the presence of multiple cookies placed on a particular computer by multiple advertisers on each web page has resulted in vast amounts of information being collected about each person and his or her online activities. For this reason, many regulations and security standards focus on **controls** for cookie usage. A single commercial web page may access or deliver several hundred cookies on behalf of several hundred organizations using a technique known as **pixel tracking**. See also **behavioral microtargeting**.

corrective action – a specific activity (triggered by an event) that when complete will result in the mitigation or resolution of a problem. The fact that the activity is triggered by an event makes it reactive and therefore corrective.

Corrective And Preventive Action system (CAPA) – an automated tracking process to ensure that key activities (actions) to resolve or mitigate gaps in security or **compliance** are consistently tracked through to completion. **CAPA** represents the actions, with **system** representing the automated processes for enforcing the manual activities that manage the resolution of those items.

corrective control – (see also **control**) a **method** of defense that is introduced as the reactive result of an observed deficiency in security. For example, the addition of greater **network segmentation** after an **attack** can be considered a corrective control.

corrupt (in the context of cybersecurity) – a condition within a **digital device** in which electronic **data** critical to the normal function has become unusable. This may mean that the device is not functioning or alternatively that the device is considered to be untrustworthy due to an **infection** acquired during a successful **malware attack**.

crack – to break into a secured **digital device**, account or service by defeating one or more security measures designed to prevent the intrusion.

credential stuffing – a high-volume form of a **password** re-use **attack**. Due to the large number of people who re-use passwords across different **systems** and **applications**, some criminals leverage usernames and passwords obtained from one source to attempt to gain access to another. This can be accomplished at high volume and high speed using automated tools. Users can prevent this type of attack from being successful simply by always using a unique password. Systems can decrease the chances of this happening when they can detect and block unusual access attempts.

crimeware – software that is intentionally designed to perform illegal acts, such as theft or ransom demands. A term for a specific subset of **malware**.

critical infrastructure – the core hardware, software and physical locations in any **digital landscape** that enables the highest-priority technology services and **data** flows to operate.

Cross-Site Request Forgery (**CSRF**) – one of the **OWASP** top 10 critical security flaws to guard against. The ability of an **attacker** to trick a user by embedding or re-using the victim's identification credentials to get a computing service to perform an unintended action. For example, by getting a user to click on a **phishing** link in an email or in an unrelated website, the attacker, without the victim's knowledge, is then able to enter another website the victim subscribes to, using the victim's log-in credentials from the email account or the unrelated website. The attacker can then perform whatever actions he or she wants to on the website he or she has just logged into. If the phishing link can be embedded in the web page of the site being targeted, it has a greater chance of success, as the user will already be **authenticate**d and the action is more likely to be considered legitimate. As examples, this technique can be used to change a registered email address or to perform a financial transaction, without the victim being aware of these actions, since the action request is embedded in the link.

Cross-Site Scripting (also known as **XSS**) – a security **exploit** that takes advantage of security design flaws in web-generated pages. If the dynamic pages from a legitimate site do not have very robust rules, users' machines can be exploited by a 3rd party that presents false links or dialog boxes that appear to be from the legitimate site, but are not. A specific instance of an XSS **vulnerability** is known as an **XSS hole**.

cryptanalysis – the art of examining **cipher**ed information to determine how to circumvent the technique that was used to encode or hide it; i.e. to analyze ciphers.

cryptocurrency – any digital version of money that makes use of **encryption** to generate and secure confidence in the units that are traded. These forms of payment are usually decentralized and unregulated, and it is difficult to trace currency owners. This makes cryptocurrency the main form of payment for **cybercrime** and **ransomware**. See also **Bitcoin** and **blockchain**.

cryptographic algorithm – the use of a mathematical and/or computational model to **cipher** information from plain text to a hidden format.

cryptography – the use of models to make information secret using **ciphers;** i.e. writing ciphers.

cryptojacking – a portmanteau of the words *cryptographic* and *hijacking*. This is a type of **cyber attack** in which some or all of the computing power of an environment is taken over (hijacked) to run **cryptographic** processes used to process **cryptocurrency** transactions or create new cryptocurrency. The hijacker makes money because he or she is paid in cryptocurrency for the computer processing he or she contributes, even though he or she effectively stole the electricity and computing power used.

cryptology – the study of models used to make information secret using **ciphers**; i.e. reading ciphers.

cryptotrojan – a form of **malware** that is designed to look initially harmless, but that seeks to perform an **attack** that involves **cipher**ing (**encrypting**) the victim's electronic information. This technique can be used in combination with other malware and **cryptographic** techniques, usually in a **ransomware** attack. See also **blended threat**.

cryptoviral extortion – the use of a specific form of **malware** that seeks to spread (install in new locations) and **cipher** (**encrypt**) the victim's information for the purpose of demanding payment for the information's release. See also **ransomware**.

cryptovirology – the study of the use of **ciphers** (**encryption** and **cryptography methods**), predominantly to understand how to build better **cyber attacks**.

cryptovirus – a form of **malware** that spreads by infecting (attaching itself to) other files and that makes use of **cryptography**, usually in the **method** by which it **attacks** a victim's electronic **data** files. The victim's files are usually **cipher**ed (**encrypted**) so that the **attacker** can demand a release fee. See also **ransomware**.

cryptoworm – a form of **malware** that actively seeks to spread to new locations and **devices** without human interaction, and that then makes use of **cryptography**, usually in the **method** by which it **attacks** a victim's electronic **data** files. The technique the **worm** uses actively seeks to identify and make use of any available communication paths or **protocols**. This is a subtype of a **cryptovirus**, and, like a cryptovirus, a cryptoworm usually **ciphers** (**encrypts**) a victim's files so that the **attacker** can demand a release fee. See also **ransomware**.

CSRF – see **Cross-Site Request Forgery**.

CVE Identifier – the acronym stands for **C**ommon **V**ulnerabilities and **E**xposures. This is a unique number assigned in a publicly accessible database for all known (and suspected) security **vulnerabilities** in publicly released software. The database is maintained by the not-for-profit US MITRE Corporation. The format used is CVE + Year + (number assigned) – so, for example, CVE-2014-6271 is the initial identifier for the **shellshock** security **bug**, with the middle number indicating it was registered in 2014. The list can be accessed through http://cve.mitre.org/

cyber – when used as a prefix, denotes that the item is relevant to computing technology, digital culture or **digital device**s.

cyber attack – an aggressive or hostile action that leverages or targets **digital devices**. The intended damage is not limited to the digital (electronic) environment.

cyber attack lifecycle – a conceptual model of the sequential steps that are involved in a successful unauthorized intrusion or disruption into a **digital landscape** or **digital device**. There are a number of models currently available; an example of the most common steps found across the models are illustrated within the definition of **advanced persistent threat**. See also **kill chain**.

cybercrime – an act that violates the laws of one or more countries through the illicit use of or access to one or more digital technologies.

cyber criminal – any person who attempts to gain **unauthorized access** to one or more **digital devices**.

cyber defense – the collective set of technologies, processes and people that act to defend any given **digital landscape**. See also **advanced threat defense**.

cyber defense points – the digital locations where **cybersecurity controls** could be added. Examples of such defense points include **data**, **applications**, **systems**, **devices** and **networks**.

cyber defense strategies – a short list of the primary defensive countermeasure types that can be considered at each stage in the **cyber attack lifecycle** as part of a structured defense. These are typically summarized as: detect, deny, disrupt, degrade, deceive and contain. See also **kill chain**.

cyber espionage – the use of digital technologies to help steal information from any organization or individual in order to create a financial or political gain.

cyber false flag – the act of a **hacker** or other **threat actor** intentionally placing misleading evidence within his or her **cyber attack** to trick investigators into making incorrect accusations during any subsequent attempt at **attribution**. Examples include launching the attack from a rival's geographic location, using the language of a rival state when writing the attack code or including blocks of code that are already attributed to another party. Often multiple pieces of fake evidence will be used in a single attack in which the perpetrator wants to mask his or her activity. False flag tactics mostly tend to be used by sophisticated hackers and nation states.

cyber forensics – see **digital forensics**.

cybergeddon – a portmanteau of the words **cyber** and Arma**geddon** (which refers to biblical references to the end of the world and in modern times is used to refer to extremely catastrophic events) – is an event with catastrophic consequences for all interconnected **digital devices** within a wide geographic area to the extent that the **digital landscape** would require substantial time and effort to rebuild. Due to the extent that society relies on digital devices, the expected impact would be the temporary disintegration of social order within the affected area.

cyber incident response – see **incident response**.

cyber insecurity – suffering from a concern that weaknesses in your **cybersecurity** are going to cause you personal or professional harm.

cyber maneuver – an action, **method** or process designed to **attack** or defend all or part of **a digital landscape** in order to gain an advantage over an adversary. The activity is designed to capture, disrupt, destroy, deny or otherwise manipulate the position of the adversary.

cyber operations – the process of gathering information about active **threats** to the **digital landscape**. Usually includes a combination of real-time **threat intelligence** about **network** and **malware attacks**, together with external intelligence about active and emerging **threats**.

cyber physical systems – real world mechanisms monitored or controlled by **digital devices** and their algorithms. Combinations of digital devices that include sensors, actuators or other mechanisms to interact with the real world (the physical component) can work together through self-learning computer-based algorithms to integrate their functions, authorized users and resources. They can use their transdisciplinary capabilities to address problems in real time. As an example – such a **system** can learn or understand how to regulate or respond to real world changes – such as a sensor reading resulting in a dynamic decision to change to a flow rate via an actuator. A component of **Industry 4.0**.

cybersecurity – the protection of **digital devices** and their communication channels to keep them stable, dependable and reasonably safe from danger or **threat**. Usually the required protection level must be sufficient to prevent or address **unauthorized access** or intervention before it can lead to substantial personal, professional, organizational, financial and/or political harm. In the UK this term is used as 2 words – **cyber security**.

cybersecurity architecture – see **security architecture**.

cybersecurity control types – categories used to help organize the defenses against **cyber attacks**. Usually, these categories are (i) technical (ii) procedural (iii) physical and (iv) **compliance**-related (or legal/contractual). Each of the **cyber defense points** should be established and in place as appropriate to the **risks** revealed by careful consideration of all of the **cyber control types**.

cyber security incident – see **security incident**.

cyberspace – the area available for electronic information to exist inside any collection of interconnected **digital devices**.

cyber threat dwell time – see **dwell time**.

cyberwar – an active campaign by one entity that has the purpose of defeating an enemy entity through disruption to, compromise of or theft from the enemy's **digital landscape**. The entity can be a nation state, company or other organization.

cyber warrior – a person who engages in attempts to gain **unauthorized access** to or seeks to disrupt **digital devices**, **systems** or **networks** for personal, political or religious reasons.

CybOX – a standard for the communication and exchange of information about *Cyber observables* related to **threat** events. See **STIX** for further information on content and usage.

D is for Dwell-Time

dark fiber – a privately owned or leased optical **data** connection (fiber optic) that can be used for communication. Although these connections were once considered to be inherently secure, multiple techniques have been developed to intercept or read communication data, even though these techniques usually require initial physical access to some part of the communication route or hardware.

dark Internet – originally referred to publicly accessible electronic **data** content that was unreadable only because of its format or indexing. For example, a store of raw scientific data may have been **Internet** accessible, but without indexing or context it was considered to be part of the dark Internet. This term is now sometimes used to mean content that is intentionally hidden, but the term **deep web is now used more commonly**. See also **Internet**.

darknet – this is effectively an encrypted, private network that exists within the **Internet** and requires specific software and knowledge to access. The darknet is used for the most extreme criminal and secretive activities. Some lesser criminal activities do not require this level of secrecy and instead use the **dark web**.

dark web – a subset of the **deep web** consisting of websites that *intentionally* hide their server locations. Such sites are not registered on standard search engines, and the hidden server values make it extremely difficult to determine which organizations and people are behind these sites. Dark web contents are usually hidden because the data, products or services they offer are illegal. The dark web is accessible through browsers such as **Tor** but unlike the **darknet**, the contents are not usually encrypted. See also **dark Internet** and **darknet**.

DAST – acronym for **D**ynamic **A**pplication **S**ecurity **T**esting. See **dynamic testing**.

data – information stored in an electronic or digital format.

data breach notification procedure – see **breach notification procedure**.

data center – any facility (building or room) that is operated as a hub for transacting or storing large amounts of electronic information. Computing **devices** within these facilities are usually arranged in racks. The size and features within each facility can vary enormously, but usually this type of facility includes controlled physical access and redundancy (failsafes) appropriate to the value of the transactions the facility is supporting. A tier system (1-4) is used to express the basic failsafe features of each data center. A *Tier 1* data center has no failsafe features and a *Tier 4* data center is required to have full redundancy to all **systems**, including power supplies, **data** links and cooling systems (**HVAC** – Heating, Ventilation and Air-

Conditioning).

data chain of custody – see **chain of custody**.

data classification – the process of arranging sets of electronic information into categories based on their value, impact, required level of secrecy and other attributes. Typical attributes for this categorization process include **confidentiality**, **integrity** (the need for the information to be un**corrupt**ed) and **availability**.

data controller – the organization that owns and is accountable for a set of **data**. As discussed in many privacy regulations around the world, the role of the data controller can have legal and financial implications for the organization and/or for a specific person (organization role) if **compliance** requirements are not met.

Data Encryption Standard (**DES**) – an early standard for **cipher**ing information from plain text to secret information using symmetrical **key**s, developed around 1975. **Triple DES** is a version of the same standard that uses a bundle of keys to help increase the strength of the ciphering, but it still offers lower security levels than more recent standards do. These **method**s are considered to be outdated (no longer effective) because it is now easy to break the **encryption**, and because DES has been replaced by other standards, including the **Advanced Encryption Standard**.

data governance – the management of electronic information through the use of **policies** and **procedures** designed to ensure that transactions and storage are handled with appropriate care. See also **data classification**.

Data Loss Prevention (**DLP**) – this term can describe both (i) the technologies and (ii) the strategies used to help stop information from being taken out of an organization without the appropriate **authorization**. Software technologies can use heuristics (patterns that fit within certain rules) to recognize, alert and/or block **data** extraction activities on **digital devices**. For example, a DLP technology may prohibit specific types of file attachments from being sent out via Internet mail services. These technologies can also prevent or monitor many other attempts at removing or copying data. There are workarounds that can be used by skilled **hackers** to evade detection by these solutions, including **encryption** and fragmentation. Although these solutions are becoming an essential line of defense, the most secure environments aim to prevent any significant set of data from being available for export in the first place. For this reason, Data Loss Prevention is often thought of as the last line of defense (a final safety net if all other security **controls** have not been successful). **Information Loss Prevention** (**ILP**) is an alternative version of the same term.

DDoS – acronym for **Distributed Denial of Service**. See **Denial of Service** for definition.

DDoS filtering – the process security technologies use to sift through any barrage of **data** requests sent as part of an **attack** to identify and allow legitimate traffic to pass, while preventing or limiting the impact of the illegitimate requests. See also **Denial of Service** for information about this attack type.

deauth – a shortened form of **deauth**orization, used to represent a form of attack where a **device** or program is forced to lose its settings to the extent where it will return to an out-of-the-box default state. If the default state has **vulnerabilities** (such as a default password) this can then be used as a **vector** for compromising the device or software program.

decapitation – (in the context of **malware**) preventing any compromised **device** from being able to communicate, receive instruction, send information or spread malware to other devices. This can effectively render many forms of malware ineffective because it removes any command, **control** or theft benefit. This is often a stage during **takedown** or **threat** removal.

deception detection – the ability to correctly identify and alert any attempt to hide or commit any fraudulent act.

deep content inspection – an advanced form of **Data Loss Prevention** technology that allows the full set of any information being processed to be reviewed against a set of updatable rules, so blocking, reporting, notification or other actions can be automatically applied. For example, a rule can be put in place so that if any set of 16-digit numbers (credit card accounts) are being sent in batches exceeding 50 from any user **device**, the action can be blocked and reported. Standard Data Loss Prevention only reviews the main headers and tags, whereas this form of prevention performs a review of all the information content. Also sometimes referred to as **adaptive content inspection** (**ACI**) or deep-level content inspection.

deep web – Internet content that cannot be seen by search engines. This includes not only **dark web** content but also harmless and general content that is not indexed or generally reachable; for example, personal databases and paid content.

default accounts – generic user and **password** permissions, often with **administrative access** that is provided as standard for some **applications** and hardware for use during initial setup. A basic **cybersecurity control** is to ensure all default accounts are disabled or at least have their passwords changed because many **cyber attacks** will seek to find and use any default accounts that were missed or forgotten.

defense by design – the process of ensuring that protective security measures are consistently included and embedded from the earliest requirements stage of any component in a **digital landscape**. Components of the digital landscape include **digital**

devices, electronic information, software **applications** and communication channels.

defense in depth – the use of multiple layers of security techniques to help reduce the chance of a successful **attack**. The idea is that if one security technique fails or is bypassed, there are others that should address the attack. The latest (and correct) thinking on defense in depth is that security techniques must also consider people and operational factors (for example processes) and not just technology.

Denial of Service (DoS) – an **attack** designed to stop or disrupt peoples' use of organizations' **systems**. Usually, a particular section of an enterprise is targeted; for example, a specific **network**, **system**, **digital device** type or function. These attacks usually originate from, and are targeted at, **devices** accessible through the Internet. If the attack is from multiple source locations, it is referred to as a **Distributed Denial of Service**, or **DDoS**, attack.

DES – acronym for **Data Encryption Standard**. See **Data Encryption Standard** for definition.

detective control – (see also **control**) a **method** of defense used to help identify items or issues that may occur but that are not being defeated or prevented by other means. For example, an **intrusion detection system** may identify and alert a new issue but may not have the means to defeat the problem without additional intervention.

device encryption – usually refers to encoding (making unreadable) the information at rest on a smartphone, tablet, laptop or other electronic item. This encoding makes the information stored on the item readable only when a valid user is logged in.

devices – any hardware used to create, modify, process, store or transmit **data**. Computers, smartphones and **USB** drives are all examples of devices.

DevOps – a portmanteau of the words *Development* and *Operations*. This term is used to describe organizations in which the development of technology is brought closer to the operational (business) needs by requiring the people, processes and technologies to work more closely together. Instead of keeping the development team separated from the business and customer functions where the solutions are used, an overall lifecycle is created with business engagement from the outset (initial design) and throughout the lifecycle in a cyclical process of continuous improvement. See also **DevSecOps**.

DevSecOps – a portmanteau of the words *Development*, *Security* and *Operations*. This term has the same meaning as **DevOps** but also includes the recognition that effective **cybersecurity** must be embedded in the same continuous lifecycle as development and operations. Specifically, security requirements should be defined at the outset of any development, and should then be tested during development (for example, through **static source testing** (also known as **SAST**) and prior to release (for example, through **penetration testing** (also known as **dynamic testing** or **DAST**), and finally, additional, appropriate security measures (such as **vulnerability scan**ning and **file integrity monitoring**) should be put in place during live usage (the production system). Static and dynamic testing can be augmented or replaced by Interactive Application Security Testing (**IAST**) or Runtime Application Security Protection (**RASP**) both of which incorporate static and dynamic testing but add capabilities to help check more parameters and can operate to identify and alert issues in real-time environments. See also **IAST** and **RASP**.

Dictionary attack – a form of **brute force attack** that attempts to crack a **cipher**, **password** or decryption key using words, phrases and expected values (such as popular passwords).

digital device – any electronic appliance that can create, modify, archive, retrieve or transmit information in an electronic format. Desktop computers, laptops, tablets, smartphones and Internet-connected home **devices** are all examples of digital devices.

digital fingerprinting – has two different potential meanings. (i) to <u>covertly</u> embed ownership information inside any form of electronic information, so that original ownership can still be established on stolen or copied information. This differs from **digital watermarking** because the ownership information is hidden. (ii) the use of characteristics that are unique to an electronic file or object to help prevent, detect or track unauthorized storage, usage or transmission. Used as a form of defense on high-sensitivity intellectual property.

digital forensics – a specialized field in which personnel help preserve, rebuild and recover electronic information and help investigate and uncover residual evidence after a **cyber attack**. See also **indicators of compromise**.

digital landscape – the collection of **digital devices** and electronic information that is visible or accessible from a particular location.

digital sentience – the development of knowledge and skills in computer programs (**applications**) so that they are self aware, can independently choose to acquire new skills and capabilities, and can express thoughts or beliefs based on observations and information acquired.

digital signature – a secure digital technology that uses a mathematical technique to verify the authenticity of an electronic signature. Digital signatures may only be considered the equivalent of their handwritten counterpart when evidence of unique access to the mathematical technique can be proved without doubt.

digital skimming – any technique used to steal a copy of a layer of electronic information (**data**). For example, through the illicit insertion of programming code (such as a **script**) into a legitimate web page so that a copy of the information entered is sent covertly to a collection point used by an **attacker**.

digital watermarking – a technique that embeds ownership information inside any form of electronic information. This technique can be used to enhance some forms of advanced **cyber defense**, especially for intellectual property, so even if it is stolen, the information will still contain evidence of the original owner. See also **digital fingerprinting**.

Disaster Recovery Plan – see **Technical Disaster Recovery Plan**.

Distributed Denial of Service (DDoS) – see **Denial of Service**.

distributed guessing – an **attack** technique that allows the jigsaw of information about a person or his or her credit card that is held or accessible across multiple websites to be assembled into enough information to perform a fraudulent transaction. This type of attack takes advantage of (i) the different pieces of available information that may be held on each website service and (ii) the ability to make multiple invalid guesses on each site, with no centralized lockout of the card or the user's personal details. Using this technique through automated tooling, an **attacker** can turn basic information such as 4 card digits and a person's name into complete credit card details, including the long card number, validity dates and security code.

diversion – the **social engineering** tactic of re-directing a potential target to a fake location designed to elicit information or transactions intended for the real destination. Re-directing a physical package at reception to a person posing as the recipient is an example of this tactic. **Pharming** (re-direction of traffic for a real website to a fake site set-up by an attacker) is also an example of the use of this technique.

DKIM – acronym for **Domain Keys Identified Mail**, a form of email **authentication** designed to help prevent **spoofing** (pretending to be a different email sender). While an email is being sent, the technique embeds a **digital signature** within the email using a private **encryption key**. The signature can then be verified by the recipient through a **public key**. This process helps any recipient verify that a message and its contents have not been modified since they were sent. Used as part of an email validation **system** known as **DMARC**. See also **DMARC**.

DLP – see **Data Loss Prevention**.

DMARC – acronym for **D**omain-based **M**essage **A**uthentication, **R**eporting and **C**onformance. This is an email validation **system** to help identify and prevent email **spoofing**. It uses **DKIM** and **SPF** (the **Senders Policy Framework**) to help **authenticate** genuine messages and allows rules to be set for handling email messages that fail any or all validity verifications.

DNS – acronym for **D**omain **N**ame **S**ystem. Whenever a **network** or Internet location uses a plain text name (such as www.cybersimplicity.com), this has to be translated into a specific and more technical location called the **IP address**. A **DNS service** runs on a server to reconcile and translate the text value into the specific network location's IP address value.

DNS service – see **DNS**.

DNS sinkhole – a **method** of detecting, blocking or re-directing traffic to a website or web page by subverting the **Domain Name System service** (**DNS service**) to provide false information. This technique is mostly used for defensive purposes. For example, this can be used to redirect internal users away from restricted or infected websites to a warning page. The main objective of this approach is to re-direct the flow of **data** from an intended target to a different location.

DNS tunneling – the use of the **domain name system protocol**, which translates **network** locations from plain text into **IP addresses**, as a method of **exfiltrating** (stealing) **data**. **Firewalls** are used to filter **DNS** information to allow legitimate requests to flow across networks. By tampering with and leveraging some of the values within the DNS protocol, information can potentially be transacted by an **attacker** hiding his or her data as DNS traffic to thereby bypass firewalls.

domain – a section of **Internet** or **network** territory. Within any **URL,** a domain usually consists of a name plus a suffix; for example *google.com* is a domain. The suffix (in this example *.com*) is often referred to as the **TLD** or top-level domain. If a domain is prefixed, for example *maps.google.com*, then the reference is considered to be to a sub-domain.

dorking – see **Google Hacking**.

DoS – see **Denial of Service**.

doxxing (also **doxing**) – publicly exposing personal information on the Internet. Thought to be based on an abbreviation of the word 'documenting.'

drive-by download – the unintended receipt of malicious software onto a **device** through an Internet page, electronic service or link. The victim is usually unaware that his or her actions permitted new malicious software to be pulled onto and installed into the **digital device** or **network**.

dronejack – a portmanteau of **drone** and hi**jack**. To take control over an autonomous (usually flight-capable) vehicle by gaining **unauthorized access** to its **control system**.

dropper – a form of **trojan** malicious software (**malware**) designed to act as a foothold for the installation of other malware. Often used during the early stages of an **APT** (advanced persistent threat) to help embed and expand the attack.

dual homed – any **network device** that has more than one network interface. The primary **method** of positioning **firewalls** and other network boundary or perimeter defenses uses this technique to connect **untrusted networks** to **trusted networks** by keeping them isolated on different network connections and applying rules and **controls** to any **data** that is passed across these connections.

dumpster diving – the **social engineering** technique of looking through the trash of a target to locate items that may contain information of value that can then be used towards a subsequent **attack**. Contents found could include items such as the victims name, address, account numbers, companies he or she deals with, etc.

dwell-time – in the context of **cybersecurity** – this refers to how long an intrusion or **threat** has been allowed to remain in place before being discovered and eliminated. The length of time between intrusion and detection is an indication of how successful an **advanced persistent threat** has been. Although the dwell-time is expected to fall as cybersecurity measures mature, the average time is hundreds of days, and in some cases the dwell-time is discovered to be years.

dynamic/adaptive access controls – technologies and processes that can increase or decrease the strength of **authentication** checks based on understanding the context, current **threat**-level and **risk** factors involved. See also **adaptive access**.

Dynamic Host Configuration Protocol (DHCP) – the standard **method** used on **networks** and the Internet to assign an address (**Internet Protocol, or IP**) to any **digital device** to allow its communications **systems** to operate. This address is assigned by a server (host) each time an authorized digital device connects to it.

dynamic testing – (in the context of **cybersecurity**) assesses the security standards and potential **vulnerabilities** within an **application** or service when it is running in an environment equivalent to the real world environment in which it will be operated (a production environment). Also known as **DAST** – **d**ynamic **a**pplication **s**ecurity **t**esting. This is usually a form of **black-box penetration testing**. See also **static testing** and **IAST**.

E is for Exploit

eavesdropping – covertly or secretly listening in on a communication.

edge computing – a **method** of improving **IoT** and **digital device** response times and **resilience** by placing the **applications** and services they rely on at the perimeter (edge) of the **network** they are being used by, instead of within, for example, a **public cloud**. See also **fog computing**.

EMM – acronym for Enterprise Mobility Management. This term is used as an umbrella to include all of the functionality and processes required by an organization to enable appropriate and secure usage of **digital devices** and connections that are expected to travel outside of their **network**. The term encompasses **Mobile Device Management (MDM)** for smartphones and tablets, together with laptop and portable **IoT** security.

employee-led cloud adoption – a form of **shadow IT** where people working for an organization take it upon themselves to start using Internet-based services without going through official routes for assessing and configuring the usage to a secure standard. See also **BYOC**.

encryption – the act of encoding messages so that if they are intercepted by an unauthorized party, they cannot be read unless the encoding mechanism can be de**cipher**ed.

endpoint – a final digital destination where electronic information is processed by users. Computers, smartphones and tablet **devices** are all examples of endpoints.

endpoint behavior analysis – analyzing unusual patterns on user **devices**, such as changes to registry entries, unusual traffic patterns or file changes, as indications of potential **threats** or other **malware-**related activity. This can contribute to **indicators of compromise threat intelligence**.

endpoint forensics – the techniques by which static and **in-memory** evidence is captured to preserve, rebuild and uncover this evidence from a known or suspected **attack** on a user **device**. See also **endpoint**.

endpoint protection – a term used to describe the collective set of security software that has become standard for most user-operated **digital devices**. The security software may include **anti-malware**, a personal **firewall**, intrusion prevention software and other protective programs and processes.

endpoint security – see **endpoint protection**.

Eternal Blue – a powerful **exploit**, originally developed by the US NSA, leaked in April 2017 and subsequently used within two major **malware**-based **cyber attacks** (**WannaCry** in May 2017 and **NotPetya** in June 2017). The exploit targeted a critical **vulnerability** in Microsoft **operating system**s that enabled infections to spread swiftly in environments that were running out-of-date operating systems or were slow to deploy patches (software updates), if they also had weak security configurations. Eternal Blue was notable because it showed how widespread the failure to implement basic good **cybersecurity** practices had become. Eternal Blue has the **CVE identifier** CVE-2017-0144.

ethical hacker – an alternative name for a **penetration tester**.

ethical hacking – the process of supportive (**white-hat**) **penetration testing** experts assisting in finding security weaknesses and **vulnerabilities**.

event – see **security event**.

exfiltrate – to move something with a degree of secrecy sufficient to not be noticed. Used to describe moving stolen **data** through detection **systems**.

exploit – to take advantage of a security **vulnerability**. Well-known exploits are often given names. Falling victim to a known exploit with a name can be a sign of low security, such as poor **patch management**.

F is for Firewall

failure to restrict URL access – originally one of the **OWASP** top 10 critical security flaws to guard against, this evolved to become the term '**missing function level access control**.' This describes a state in which a web-based **application** will respond to a request in a link (**URL**) without verifying that it is from a valid and known source.

fake website – can either be (i) a fraudulent imitation of a real Internet page or site that is designed to look like one from the legitimate company, or (ii) an Internet page or site from a completely fake company, often with a 'too good to be true' offer or misleading content. In both instances, the objectives of the site may include capturing genuine log-in credentials, receiving real payments for orders that will not be delivered, or installing **malware**.

false negative – in the context of **cybersecurity**, this is where a legitimate security problem is identified as harmless when it should have been identified as an issue or problem that required correction or attention. The opposite of **true negative**.

false positive – in the context of **cybersecurity**, this is where a security person or technology incorrectly identifies something as a security issue when it is not. The rate of false positives is regarded as a significant security metric. A lower false positive rate indicates that fewer legitimate transactions are being flagged as security issues. The opposite of **true positive**.

fat client – a computer program requiring installation on an end **device** such as a laptop, tablet, smartphone or other computer. This term contrasts with **applications** that do not require installation (for example, those that work through **web browser**s), and are known as **thin client**. In application architecture, the client is the piece of a computer program in which the end user interacts with the program interface.

file integrity monitoring – **method**s and technologies used to ensure that the contents of any particular electronic **data** set are kept exactly as they are expected to be. Any unexpected or unauthorized changes can trigger an automatic alert and/or the restoration of the file based on whatever rules are set to operate.

fileless malware – is a form of malicious software (**malware**) **attack** that seeks to remain hidden by using techniques that avoid placing artifacts (files) on the storage area of a **digital device**. Instead, the attack seeks opportunities to append itself to legitimate services that operate in the **memory** (the **RAM**) of the target device. If an attack does not make any detectable changes to the file storage area and an organization is only running older security technologies that are not monitoring the activity in the memory (the **in-memory** area), the attack can be very difficult to detect. This is because only legitimate and expected services may appear to be running.

file transfer protocol (**FTP**) – the standard **method** used to send and receive packages of information (files). **SFTP**, or **secure file transfer protocol,** is the secure variation of this method that is used to send and receive **data** through an **encrypted** connection. Even if data is sent through an encrypted connection, it will not itself be automatically encrypted. See also **MFT** for managed file transfer.

fingerprinting – see **digital fingerprinting**.

firewall – is hardware (physical **device**) or software (computer program) used to monitor and protect inbound and outbound **data** (electronic information). It achieves this by applying a set of rules. These physical devices or computer programs are usually deployed, at a minimum, at the perimeter of each **network** access point. Software firewalls can also be deployed on devices to add further security. The rules applied within a firewall are known as the **firewall policy**. Advanced firewalls are often equipped with other defensive features typical of more **unified threat management**.

firewall policy – the rules applied within either a physical hardware **device** (a hardware **firewall**) or **software program** (a software firewall) to allow or block specific types of inbound and outbound **data** traffic at the perimeter of a **network** or **digital**

device.

fog computing – the positioning of distributed and federated computational power with lower latency (faster response time) than standard **cloud** computing to support improved service and **resilience** for **smart** end **devices**. Differs from **edge computing** in that the placement of the computational power is not necessarily inside or at the periphery of a **network**. Rather than a small number of very large **data center**s that may be used by a service such as a **public cloud**, a large number of smaller units can be placed in closer proximity to where the processing power is required. Frequently, fog computing does not fully replace the use of larger cloud facilities but can be used to help speed up real-time responses, with the results still passed back to larger facilities for deeper analysis and processing.

footprinting – a technique used by both **attackers** and security testers to obtain information about the computer **systems**, access points, **ports** and services belonging to a specific site or organization. This information can then be used to either help improve security by taking measures to hide the footprint, or, if used by an attacker, to ascertain potential **vulnerabilities** to **exploit**.

forensics – see **digital forensics**.

FTP – see **file transfer protocol**.

fuzzing – this term has 2 potential definitions; (1) in the context of **cybersecurity**, this is a portmanteau of **fuzz** and testing to describe a **method** of software testing that involves entering random, unexpected, invalid and out-of-range **data** as inputs into a program. The software is then checked for any **memory** leaks, crashes or other flaws that result from these inputs. This can help to identify and address potential security **vulnerabilities**. This technique may also be used by **threat actors** as part of a **cyber attack**, to exploit any memory leak

vulnerability that has not been adequately secured within any component within a **digital landscape**. (2) There is also a **social engineering** technique of the same name (fuzzing) that involves overloading a person with information so that they become more amenable to defer to calculations or decisions made by the attacker.

fuzz test – see **fuzzing**.

G is for Governance

garbage code – a technique used by some forms of **malware** to intentionally add large volumes of **encrypted** and irrelevant programming code to make the work of defeating the **threat** more difficult. An **attacker** can hide a very small malicious **software program** inside a much larger encrypted file (potentially thousands or millions of times larger), making the process of **quarantine**, decryption and elimination of the threat much harder.

gateway – a point in a **network** that can be used to pass into another network. This location is a key target for **cyber attacks** and network level defenses.

geo-location – a portmanteau of *geographic location*. In the context of **cybersecurity**, this is the use of information about the physical position (such as the country or town) from which a request (such as an access request or credit card transaction) has originated. This information can be used to help **authenticate** valid transactions and block rogue requests. Automatic correlation and analysis of this type of information can also be used to raise alerts or block invalid requests. For example, a request from a user travelling to a different country, followed by a request a few seconds later from a completely different country, can be automatically detected and blocked. Geo-location is considered a valuable source of **data** for the detection and prevention of **cyber attacks**.

Google dorking – alternative name for **Google hacking**. See **Google hacking**.

Google hacking – the use of search engines and other public **applications** and services by **attackers** to identify security gaps that can be **exploited** in a specific target. Originally, the type of easily-exploited **vulnerabilities** that were identified through this **method** led to the victims being regarded as 'dorks' or '**Google dork**s.' This was because the vulnerabilities could be located through a standard search engine due to the victims failing to incorporate basic security configurations. In the context of **social engineering**, this term may also refer to acquiring personal information about a potential victim through the information about them that is available over the public Internet – not necessarily only through or via the Google search engine.

governance – the **method**s used by any executive to keep his or her organization on track with the management goals and within acceptable performance standards. This is usually achieved by establishing **policies**, **procedures** and **controls** that match the enterprise's vision, strategy and **risk** appetite.

governance, risk and compliance – a term used to describe the interaction and interdependence between the activities that (i) control any organization (**governance**) (ii) verify and enforce those **controls** (**compliance**) and (iii) manage any substantial exposures to financial impact that emerge (**risk**), often due to gaps in (i) and/or (ii).

grey hat – a **hacker** who does not have the overt, unethical intentions of a **black hat**, but still makes use of techniques and tactics that are illegal. This type of hacker intends to make use of some unethical practices to help deliver ethical goals. See also **white hat**.

grid computing – a **network** of **digital devices** that openly share their resources with each other. A grid computer is effectively a **supercomputer** that can perform significant tasks by leveraging a large number of smaller and distributed computers.

H is for Hacker

hack – the act of gaining **unauthorized access** to a **digital device**, **network**, **system**, account or other electronic **data** repository.

hacker – a person who engages in attempts to gain **unauthorized access** to one or more **digital devices**, **networks**, **systems**, accounts or other electronic **data** repositories. Can be **black hat** (unethical), **grey hat** (ethical but uses some illegal tactics) or **white hat** (ethical) hacker, depending on the person's intent.

hacktivism – an amalgamation of **hacker** and activism. Describes the act of seeking **unauthorized access** into any **digital device** or **digital landscape** to promote a social or political agenda. Usually the unauthorized access is used to cause destruction, disruption and/or publicity. Individuals participating in these acts are called **hacktivists**.

hacktivist – an amalgamation of the words **hacker** and activist. Describes any individual who participates in **hacktivism**.

hardware – any physical device used for computational processing in a computing environment. Any computing device that has physical, three dimensional presence in the real world.

hashing – using a mathematical function to convert any block or group of **data** into a fixed-length value (usually shorter than the original data) that represents the original data. This fixed-length value can be used for fast indexing of large files by computer programs without the need to manage the larger data block. It is also used extensively in the field of security; for example, **digital forensics** can use this technique to verify that the data content of a copy of any examined data is identical to the original source.

Heartbleed – was the name given to the most significant security **vulnerability** (software flaw that could be taken advantage of) of its time (2012), affecting a large number (estimated at 17%) of Internet servers that used **openSSL cryptography**. It allowed **hackers** to steal private **encryption keys**, user **cookies** and **passwords** from vulnerable Internet servers. A patch to fix the flaw was released on the day the vulnerability was publicly disclosed in 2014. It was given the **CVE identifier** CVE-2014-0160.

hodl – acronym for 'Hold On for Dear Life,' used by some members of the **Bitcoin** and **cryptocurrency** community to reflect their investment attitude to retain their currency through substantial market highs and lows – and to think optimistically about the potential long-term value.

honey network – the collective name for a cluster of **honeypots** that operate together to help form part of a **network** intrusion detection strategy.

honeypot – an electronic device or collection of **data** that is designed to trap would-be **attackers** by detecting, deflecting or otherwise counteracting their efforts. Designed to look like a real part of an enterprise's **attack** surface, the honeypot will contain nothing of real value to the attacker, but will contain tools to identify, isolate and trace any intrusion.

host based – describes a situation in which something is installed immediately on the **device** it is protecting, servicing or subverting.

Host-based Intrusion Prevention Systems (HIPS) – a version of an **intrusion prevention system** that is installed directly onto the **digital device** it is protecting from exploitation. See also **intrusion prevention system** for a description of its purpose.

host-forensics – a **method** of capturing both static and **in-memory** evidence to preserve, rebuild and uncover evidence from a known or suspected **attack** on any **digital device**.

HTTPS – see **SHTTP**.

HVAC – acronym for **H**eating, **V**entilation and **A**ir-**C**onditioning. Some of the environmental controls used in any **data center**.

Hyper Text Transfer Protocol (HTTP) – is the standard **method** used to send information (files, pictures and other **data**) over the world wide web. HTTPS or **SHTTP** is the secure version of this **protocol** that can be used when the information requires a secure connection. It is rumored that some organizations have already or may soon be able to break the security for https/shttp.

hypervisor – a **software program** that operates as a **virtual machine** manager and monitor to create, run and monitor virtual machines. A computer on which a hypervisor operates is known as a host machine, and the virtual versions are known as guest machines. The hypervisor exists to ensure that guest machines have sufficient and efficient physical resources allocated to them. See also **virtual machine**.

I is for Indicators Of Compromise (IOC)

IaaS – acronym meaning **I**nfrastructure **a**s **a S**ervice. This is a form of **cloud** solution where, instead of owning and running a physical **network** with physical servers and other hardware, the customer is offered a solution that emulates the attributes of a physical network and server infrastructure. The cloud provider operates virtualization software to offer fast, easy, infrastructure scalability at a lower cost. Ultimately, this solution still runs on physical machines maintained by the cloud provider. The cloud provider achieves the lower cost by running a much higher automation rate and utilization of the physical hardware than customers can accomplish independently.

IAM – alternative version of the acronym for **IDAM**. See **IDAM**.

IAST – acronym for **I**nteractive **A**pplication **S**ecurity **T**esting. An advanced form of checking software for deficiencies and vulnerabilities by using a wider range of information about the software than some other testing techniques. Whereas **static testing** (**SAST**) looks only at the source code, or **dynamic testing** (**DAST**) looks from the outside in, IAST seeks to understand all of this and more. This form of testing will usually inspect the runtime environment, database connections, backend communications, third-party components, http requests, libraries and framework in use. This is achieved by deploying small programs (agents) within and around the application components. This technique allows for faster and more detailed results and can also enable testing to take place both during development and even production (when the application is in use). However, this also has the downside that it usually impacts the speed and performance of the application. See also **RASP**.

IDaaS – acronym for **Id**entity **as a S**ervice. The use of an **authentication** infrastructure that is hosted by a third party in an externally hosted solution.

IDAM – acronym for **Identity & Access Management**. The collection of processes and technologies used to manage, confirm, monitor and control legitimate access to **systems** by authorized accounts. This includes measures to ensure each access request is from a verified, expected and legitimate person or entity.

identity and access controls – the **method**/s of regulating how each person and computer service is confirmed to be who they claim to be (**authentication**) and how their permissions are regulated. See also **IDAM**.

Identity & Access Management – see **IDAM**.

IDPS – see **Intrusion Detection and Prevention System**.

ILP – see **Data Loss Prevention**.

image steganography – to conceal information inside a picture (image file) so that the initial recipient/s may not know that the message is present. Only the intended recipient is expected to know how to read the information. Used within **cyber attacks** to help hide unauthorized or unwanted communications. For example, the **Zeus malware** used an image file to communicate command and **control** instructions to the malware as **least significant bits** within a landscape image file. The recipient could only see an image file, but the malware could read the concealed message. See also **steganography** and **steganalysis**.

incident – see **security incident**.

incident prediction – the use of advanced analytics to review patterns in order to foresee the most likely impending points of failure, disruption or intrusion. This can help to promote proactive enhancements in defense or to enhance preparations for a specific type of **incident** recovery.

incident response – a prepared set of processes that should be triggered when any known or suspected event takes place that could cause material damage to an organization. The typical stages are (i) verify the event is real and identify the affected areas, (ii) contain the problem (usually by isolating, disabling or disconnecting the affected pieces), (iii) understand and eradicate the root cause, (iv) restore the affected components to their fixed state and (v) review how the process went to identify improvements that should be made. An incident response may also be required to trigger other response **procedures**, such as a **breach notification procedure**, if there is any information which has been lost that is subject to a notification requirement. For example, the loss of any personal information beyond what might be found in a phone book entry is usually considered to be a notifiable event. Now commonly referred to as part of the **SIEM** process (**S**ecurity **I**ncident and **E**vent **M**anagement).

indicators of compromise (**IOC**) – is a term originally used in computer **forensics** to describe any observable behaviors and patterns (such as particular blocks of **data**, registry changes, **IP address** references) that strongly suggest that a computer intrusion has occurred or is taking place. The collation of these patterns and behaviors are now actively used in **advanced threat defense** to help more rapidly identify potential security issues from across a monitored **digital landscape**.

industrial control systems – see **control systems**.

Industry 4.0 – the use of advanced technologies, such as **cloud computing** and distributed **Internet of Things devices** to deliver adaptable manufacturing and services at scale. The modular, intelligent and flexible nature of the approach permits continuous dynamic adjustment and improvement of the items that contribute to the end product or service. See also **cyber**

physical systems.

infection – (in the context of **cybersecurity**), unwanted invasion by an outside agent that an **attacker** uses to create damage or disruption.

information classification – the assignment of one or more values to a collection of knowledge that help us understand how alike it is to any other set of knowledge. For information security, this is usually achieved by assigning values against **confidentiality**, **integrity** and **availability**, or CIA. A fourth category, **consent**, is also sometimes used when the set of knowledge includes information on private individuals. This assignment of categories can then be used to more easily select the security and recovery approach appropriate to the information value and impact. **Data classification** is a subset of information classification, as it only includes electronic information, whereas information classification includes any form of information, including paper and other physical formats.

Information Loss Prevention [ILP] – see **Data Loss Prevention**.

information systems – see **systems**.

inherent risk – the level of exposure to loss, or the impact something has, before any mitigating **controls** are taken into consideration. For example, holding credit card **data** in a **system** brings an inherent risk to the system. See also **residual risk**.

injection – one of the **OWASP** top 10 critical security flaws to guard against. A type of **attack** that sends an unauthorized command, instruction or other **data** into a **software program** through a route or process that should be blocked. For example, an **SQL injection**, in which content is erroneously sent into a SQL database, might involve sending an unexpected string of characters into an expected webpage response. The unexpected set of information is designed to be misread so that after the expected response is processed, the additional characters form an instruction to put additional data into part of the database. This can **corrupt** the database or insert invalid values.

in-line – to place an active security defense measure directly in the path of its potential adversary. For example, to place a **DDoS** filter in the path of all web traffic, so that all this traffic has to pass through it. This has the advantage of being able to respond to and immediately manage any active **threat**; however, the disadvantage is that it can potentially slow down legitimate transactions. The opposite approach is referred to as **out-of-band**. See also **out-of-band**.

in-memory – any **digital device** can contain more than one type of **data** storage. Information that is not in active use can be stored to a **device** such as a hard disk. Information that is being used (or imminently expected to be used) by the **processor** in a computer is managed through a more active storage area (the **memory** or **active memory**). When a digital device image is captured for **digital forensic** examination, it is usual to snapshot not only the static information on any hard disk (or equivalent), but also the active information (the information **in-memory**).

insecure cryptographic storage – one of the **OWASP** top 10 critical security flaws to guard against. To not **encrypt** (**cipher**) information that should be kept secret or to use a breakable or invalid technique to cipher the information.

insecure deserialisation – one of the **OWASP** top 10 critical security flaws to guard against. This flaw occurs when a reference to an object or item that should be secret information can be guessed or calculated because of the **method** used to generate its identification reference. This technique has often been used in **replay attack**s and **privilege escalation**.

insecure direct object references – one of the **OWASP** top 10 critical security flaws to guard against. To **exploit** a software **application vulnerability** by modifying a value that **controls** access to a set of **data**, so the **attacker** gains access to the data without providing a valid **authorization**. For example, a banking application vulnerability might make it easy for an attacker to adjust the parameters of the 'ShowBalance[accountnumber]' code that allows an account holder to request a display of a bank account balance simply by changing the [accountnumber] variable, so the attacker could view other account balances.

insufficient logging and monitoring – one of the **OWASP** top 10 critical security flaws to guard against. Since **attackers** rely on their attempts evading detection, this type of security flaw can occur when, for example, a web-based **application** (an application that is accessed through a **web browser**) fails to record and alert activities that can reasonably be expected to occur in a location where **attack** activity can be detected. The counteraction to resolve this flaw is not only to record (log) the activities, but also to ensure that the information is actively reviewed for suspicious activities and to escalate any suspicions to the **incident response** (**SIEM**) process.

insufficient transport layer protection – one of the **OWASP** top 10 critical security flaws to guard against. Neglecting to put adequate security on **network** communications. Frequently, only initial **authentication** communications are **encrypted** using **SSL/TLS** security measures, leaving other communications open to being compromised.

integrity – a value that can be assigned to a set of information to indicate how sensitive it is to degradation of accuracy (such as unauthorized modification) or **data** loss. Loss in this context is about losing information without the ability for anyone to recover it from the **system** it was entered into (it is not about theft). Often this value is expressed or translated into a scale of time. For example, data with the highest possible integrity rating could be given a value of 'no data loss permitted.' If it were permitted to lose up to 4 hours of data that had been processed, the value would be '4 hours.' Usually, if any data loss is permitted, it means that there will be other processes in place to address the loss of the electronic information. The integrity value assigned to any system or **application** is used to set the frequency that the information is subject to **backup**, or in very sensitive systems with no data loss permitted, establishes the need for a permanent secondary failover system.

Internet – a globally connected set of computer systems hosting public and private content. The Internet can be considered a vast global network of computers with four different layers. (i) The **surface web** is the part of the Internet that is fully public and easy to access through standard search engines, (ii) the **deep web** is also publically accessible but has content that is generally not easy to find because it is not indexed or easy to locate (iii) the **dark web** consists of content and sites that intentionally hide their activities from view through the public Internet and (iv) the **darknet** is a private and encrypted network requiring specialist software and knowledge to access.

Internet of Things (IoT) – the incorporation of electronics into everyday items sufficient to allow them to **network** (communicate) with other network-capable **devices**. For example, to include electronics in a home thermostat so that it can be operated and can share information over a network connection to a smartphone or other network-capable device.

Internet Protocol – is the set of rules used to send or receive information from or to a location on a **network**, including information about the source, destination and route. Each electronic location (host) has a unique address (the **IP address**) that is used to define the source and the destination.

Intrusion Detection and Prevention Systems (IDPS) –

computer programs that monitor and inspect electronic communications that pass through them, with the purpose and ability (i) to block and log (record) key information about any known malicious or otherwise unwanted streams of information and (ii) to log and raise alerts about any other traffic that is suspected (but not confirmed) to be of a similar nature. These are usually placed in the communication path to allow the IDPS to prevent unwanted information from entering or leaving a **network** by dropping or blocking **packets**. IDPS can also clean some electronic **data** to remove any unwanted or undesirable packet components.

Intrusion Detection Systems (IDS) – computer programs that monitor and inspect electronic communications that pass through them, with the purpose to detect, log (record) and raise alerts on any suspected malicious or otherwise unwanted streams of information. IDS are a variation of **Intrusion Detection and Prevention Systems**, as they have no ability to block the activity; they only monitor, inspect and alert.

Intrusion Prevention Systems (IPS) – see **Intrusion Detection and Prevention Systems**. A slight variation in IPS, compared to **IDPS**, is that IPS may not collect any detection information and may only serve to block (prevent) unwanted traffic based on direct rules or instructions they receive.

IOC – see **indicators of compromise**.

IoT – see **Internet of Things**.

IP address – see **Internet Protocol**.

IPS – see **Intrusion Prevention Systems**.

IRC – acronym for **I**nternet **R**elay **C**hat, a small computer program that allows chat servers and other computers to communicate with very low bandwidth (low data demands). IRC is widely used as a method for **botnets** to communicate with their **command and control servers** and for those servers to communicate with their **bot masters**.

ISACA – the **I**nformation **S**ystems **A**udit and **C**ontrol **A**ssociation, a non-profit information security organization that manages many of the leading global security education programs, certifications and frameworks.

J is for Java

Java – a programming language designed primarily for Internet programs.

John the Ripper – a **password-cracking** tool included within the **Kali Linux** toolsets.

jump drive – a portable electronic **data** storage **device** usually attachable through a **USB port**.

K is for Kill Chain

Kali Linux – an **operating system** designed and configured with hundreds of specialized tools to support **digital forensics**, **penetration testing** (**ethical hacking**) and other capabilities to **crack** and **hack** components and services within digital environments.

kernel – the core part of the **operating system** of any **digital device**. Frequently targeted during most **cyber attack**s due to the level of **control** it has over each device. Many security techniques focus on hardening the security of the kernel. **Exploit**s target the kernel because it functions continuously in a computer's **memory system**s and monitors and controls many activities performed by digital devices. Gaining a foothold in the kernel therefore allows **hacker**s to control many aspects of a device's operating system.

key – (in the context of **cybersecurity**) is a set of information that can be used to encode or decode **encrypted** information.

keylogging – a form of malicious software that is used to record and disclose entries on a **digital device**. This type of **malware** is often used to collect credit card details, user identities and **passwords**.

key management – the protection, storage, organization and issuance of **cryptographic key**s within an organization, sufficient to allow its **encryption systems** to be operated safely and effectively. Without the ability to correctly provide encryption keys to the right people and services at the right time, the **ciphered** information will either become inaccessible to the right people, or accessible to the wrong people.

key pair – see **asymmetric cryptography**.

kill chain – a conceptual **cyber defense** model that uses the structure of **attack** as a model to build a cyber defense strategy. The stages in an **advanced persistent threat** are typically used as a framework, with **cyber defense strategies** (detect, deny, disrupt, degrade, deceive, contain) considered at each stage. The model works on the premise that the earlier in the lifecycle that an attack can be detected and defeated, the lower the cost incurred and damage will be. This model can be a useful adjunct to a defense strategy, but also has inherent gaps; for example, it works best for internal organizational **networks**, but is less effective when applied to information outside of a defended perimeter. The model does, however, very successfully emphasize that **cyber attacks** are much less expensive to deal with when they are identified earlier in the **cyber attack lifecycle**.

kleptography – the study of **asymmetric backdoors** and other mechanisms that **cyber attackers** use to steal or hide information or access.

kompromat – based on the Russian term for acquiring compromising material about a victim so that they can be coerced (blackmailed) into performing actions for the **attacker**. A form of **social engineering**.

L is for Logic Bomb

laser phishing – a form of **social engineering** that uses **artificial intelligence** (**AI**) to run **botnets** capable of profiling people to target them using communication tactics designed to appeal to their personal interests, attitudes and preferences. For example, the use of AI can allow a botnet to understand the language preferences, beliefs and needs of the victim to engineer an electronic communication that is more convincing and compelling than if a lifelong friend had written it. The communication is still designed to dupe the recipient into accepting a **drive-by download**, revealing secret information or performing inadvisable tasks (such as making a bank transfer). See also **behavioral microtargeting** and **psychographics**.

latency – the delay time between sending a request and receiving a response. A lower latency means that the response time is faster (the delay is shorter). Latency (the speed of response) is a key driver for the use of more distributed computational services, such as **fog computing**.

least privilege – a basic security access practice of granting each person or user account the minimum amount of **access rights** required to perform their role.

least significant bits – the part of a binary message furthest to the right (for example 1001001), sometimes used as one **method** of concealing information in **steganography** (the concealing of hidden messages).

legal control – (in the context of **cybersecurity**) the use of legislation to help promote and invest in positive security **method**s and also to deter, punish and correct infringements.

logic bomb – a type of malicious software (**malware**) that only starts to operate when specific conditions are met. For example, when a particular date is reached.

log management – the **method** of managing the significant volume of computer-generated files, such as event logs and **audit** trails, so that they are appropriately captured, collated, analyzed and archived.

M is for Malware

MAC address – abbreviation for media access control **address**. This is a unique identifier assigned to every single **digital device** with a **network interface controller**. If a device has multiple controllers, it may have multiple (unique) addresses, one for each controller. If the identifier (MAC address) is assigned by the manufacturer, part of it will include the manufacturer's identification number. There are several related format conventions in existence. The identifier is used in **network**

(including Internet) communications.

machine learning – the ability of a **software program** to review sets of information and extrapolate theories or patterns that were not pre-programmed. This is essentially an advanced form of pattern recognition fused with an early type of **artificial intelligence**. The ability of such programs to review and understand much larger sets of electronic information than humans can handle, together with their ability to identify new trends and patterns and to then propose new findings or opportunities, makes them useful in **cybersecurity**. However, machine learning is proving to be sometimes beneficial and sometimes controversial. Two issues that have come up are that machine learning can reflect the bias or quality of the **data** and that it lacks the ethics of a human review. For example, a machine learning program designed to review fraud proposed profiling each claimant's country of origin as an indicator of the likelihood of fraud. As with other forms of statistical analysis, care must be taken with how the program interprets correlations; if a key data point is missing, the wrong conclusion can be drawn, and a correlation can be interpreted to imply causality. As a simple example - do I live in a certain country because I am overweight, am I overweight because I live in a certain country, or what other undisclosed factors may be involved?

macro virus – a form of malicious software designed to operate from within files used by other (usually legitimately installed) programs. For example, a word processing or spreadsheet file can contain sets of malicious instructions, and, if opened, these instructions will be run by the word processing or spreadsheet software. This bypasses the opportunity for **anti-malware** to detect any new software installation, as the macro virus is leveraging and subverting an **application** that is already in place.

MAC spoofing – impersonating the unique identifier (**MAC address**) of another **network interface controller**.

malspam – the use of unsolicited communications over email or other communication channels to deliver **malware**. See also **phishing**.

malvertising – a portmanteau of the words **ma**licious ad**vertising**. The use of adverts to spread **malware;** for example, by placing infected advertisements inside legitimate advertising **network**s with the capability to perform a **drive-by download** to non-secure tablets, smartphones, laptops and other **endpoint devices**.

malware – shortened version of **ma**licious soft**ware**. A term used to describe disruptive, subversive or hostile programs that can be inserted onto a **digital device**. People can intentionally or unintentionally make these types of programs harmful. Intentionally-harmful versions are usually disguised or embedded in a file that looks harmless so the **attacker** who uses them can intentionally compromise a device. Malware that someone does not intend to be harmful can still disrupt a device or leak information; however, the harmful qualities can result from unintentionally poor construction quality, bad design or insecure configuration. There are many types of malware; **adware, botnets, computer viruses, ransomware, scareware, spyware, trojans** and **worms** are all examples of intentional malware. **Hackers** often use malware to mount **cybersecurity attacks**.

MAM – acronym for **M**obile **A**pplication **M**anagement. The security process and technology for controlling or restricting which **applications** can be installed to a mobile **device** (such as a smartphone) and/or for limiting the functionality within certain installed **software program**s. For example, depending on the application's capabilities, the technology can be used to prevent users from accessing excessive numbers of records, or can restrict them to viewing (but not downloading) information. This technology can also be used to monitor application usage and suspicious behavior. Whereas **mobile device management (MDM)** focuses on security measures applied to the device, MAM focuses primarily on restricting applications and their usage and local permissions.

man-in-the-browser – a form of **malware attack** that modifies transactions within the **web browser** of the machine it is hosted on, so that covert additional transactions or transaction content can be modified without the victim's knowledge or **consent**.

man-in-the-middle – the interception and relay by a third party of selected content between two legitimate parties, for the purpose of hijacking or adjusting an electronic transaction. For example, party 1 believes he or she has connected to his or her banking home page, but is actually viewing an emulated screen offered by the intercepting **attacker**. As the login information is provided, the attacker sets up a separate connection to the bank (party 2), and is then able to respond to any challenge made by the bank by passing the same challenge back to the user (party 1). Once authorized in the transaction **system**, the attacker can then make transactions that have not been sanctioned by the user, without the user's immediate knowledge.

man-in-the-mobile – a form of **malware** for mobile phones that steals information and credentials.

MAR – in the context of cybersecurity, this is an acronym for **M**alware **A**nalysis **R**eport. A structured record or document that identifies particular attributes about an item of malicious software (**malware**). This can include how it operates (objectives), file characteristics, what software and **device**s it works on (dependencies), what **vulnerabilities** it leverages, how it behaves, how it can be neutralized and so forth.

master boot record – the first sector on any electronic **device** that defines which **operating system** should be loaded when it is initialized or re-started.

materiality – to have a level of significance or magnitude to be of concern.

md5 hash – is a very clever algorithm that can be run against any block of **data** (electronic information) to produce a unique 32 character hexadecimal (numbers and letters) identifier. If even a single character or piece of data in the block is changed, the hexadecimal identifier changes significantly. Only completely identical data blocks can ever create the same 32 character hexadecimal code. This allows for a wide range of security usages; for example, very large volumes of information (such as a forensically examined copy of a hard disk) can be compared to the original capture of the disk image and be shown to be completely as it was, without the need to do anything more than verify that the 32 digit hexadecimal value is the same as it was.

MDM – see **mobile device management**.

megabreach – when the result of a **cyber attack** involves such a high level of catastrophic theft and/or such extensive intrusion that it leads to worldwide press exposure. As the frequency and scale of breaches have increased, the threshold for newsworthy events has also increased.

Meltdown – a major, headline-making **vulnerability** discovered to impact a number of Intel, IBM and ARM computer **processor**s, with the potential to allow exploited processors to read information from within the computer **memory**. Although patches were rapidly developed by the relevant manufacturers, implementing the patches was initially estimated to slow processor speeds for some functions by between 5 and 30%. The vulnerability was issued the **CVE identifier** of CVE-2017-5754. Two similar vulnerabilities were revealed at the same time under the name **Spectre**, with wider impact to future microprocessor design.

memory – see **in-memory**.

mesh computing – a self-organizing, decentralized **method** of using all available resources to perform computing calculations. Instead of having centralized **data centers** (for example - **public cloud**) or distributed facilities (for example - **fog computing**), this method of arranging resources is designed to be fully decentralized and to offer high **resilience**, low **latency** and **supercomputer** levels of processing by using the parallel processing power available in **devices** local to the processing requirement. For example, by using a small program on every computing device, available processing time can be diverted to any task requiring that resource.

message modification – a form of **attack** in which the header information (addressee details) in a communication is changed.

metamorphic malware – a more sophisticated form of **malware** that changes all key parts of its code on each installation. **Polymorphic malware** uses fewer transformation techniques than this type of (metamorphic) malware does, as polymorphic malware usually only changes some key parts of its profile, but retains the same core **virus**. See also **blended threat**.

metaverse – technologies such as **augmented** or **virtual reality** whose artificial components create environments that are more appealing and exciting than full reality to the people who choose to exist in them. The human impact of metaverse is viewed as one of the most significant challenges and changes for humankind over the next 20 years. As an example, it is likely that metaverse participants will have a higher propensity to form what they may consider to be more satisfying and less demanding personal relationships with synthetic constructions rather than with other real people.

method – see **attack method**.

MFT – acronym for **M**anaged **F**ile **T**ransfer. A method of transporting files between locations with greater security features than basic transfer techniques such as **ftp**. For example, the additional security features of MFT can include more sophisticated access and permission control, an audit trail of activities, techniques for **non-repudiation** and functionality for **file integrity monitoring**.

micro-segmentation – a form of **containerization** where services, applications and **device**s have their components **access** isolated (i) at the most granular level possible (ii) restricted to the **least privilege**s possible and (iii) where even those privileges are only granted after verifying the trustworthiness of the component. The objective is to prevent any untrustworthy interaction by ensuring any compromised component will be extremely restricted in how it can subsequently escalate any problems or infections to other components in the **digital landscape** it exists within. Used within a **zero trust** security model. See also **zero trust**.

MIM – acronym that can mean either Mobile Identity Management or Mobile Information Management. See each term for the relevant definition.

Mirai – the first of a new type of **botnet malware** that targeted non-secure **Internet of Things (IoT) devices** that shipped with hard-coded usernames and **password**s. The malware could be easily added to the non-secure **digital devices** to form an army that **hackers** could use to perform new scales of **Distributed Denial of Service (DDoS) attacks**. See also **botnet**.

missing function level access control – one of the **OWASP** top 10 critical security flaws to guard against. Omitting adequate security **controls** to prevent instructions from being sent into a **software program** without adequate **authentication**.

mixed reality – a budget form of **augmented reality** that uses **virtual reality** to combine the virtual and real world. Instead of viewing the real world through transparent lenses with digital content overlaid (true augmented reality), mixed reality devices uses screens to show a representation of both the real and virtual images together. The visual content in mixed reality can be the same as in augmented reality but the difference is that the *real world* components are projections on a screen. See **augmented reality**.

MMS – acronym for **M**ultimedia **M**essage **S**ervice, the **protocol** used to send messages of more than 160 text characters, or to send non-text content, such as pictures, video or sound files between mobile phones.

Mobile Device Management (MDM) – a technology used to securely control the operation and use of mobile **devices** such as tablets and smartphones. Able (for example) to remotely wipe information from a mobile device and control which **applications** and functions are permitted to be installed or run.

Mobile Identity Management – software and processes that permit the identity of the users of mobile **devices** to be appropriately **authenticated**. Devices used away from the workplace can be at higher **risk** of compromise, and additional security checks to ensure the identity of the user is current, valid, and is not demonstrating anomalous behavior can help reduce this exposure.

Mobile Information Management – software and processes for maintaining the security of sensitive electronic information that belongs to an enterprise and is processed or stored through the **digital devices** that are permitted to travel and leave the enterprise's **network**.

mobile security – the specific defensive and protective practices required on portable **digital devices**. Such devices require additional considerations compared to static devices, due to the greater potential for theft and the increased diversity of the environments and connections they make. **MDM** (above) is an example of a mobile security-specific technology.

Moore's Law – created in 1965 by Gordon E. Moore. It states that over the history of computing, the processing power of computers doubles approximately every two years.

moving target defense – the use of frequent changes to multiple dimensions of a **digital landscape**'s parameters and settings, to help decrease the potential for successful **attack**.

MPLS – acronym for **M**ultiprotocol **L**abel **S**witching. A **method** used for connecting together different **networks** that are usually geographically separate, using a simple, basic and high-capacity connection. It is the network equivalent of setting up a fixed landline between two (or more) locations; however, there is very little inherent security in this connection type unless the right **security architecture** is implemented.

multi-factor authentication – using more than one form of proof to confirm the identity of a person or **device** attempting to request access. The three most widely-usedtypes of **authentication** are: (i) something you know [often a **password**] (ii) something you have [perhaps a security token or access card] and (iii) something you are [the use of **biometrics**; for example a fingerprint or facial recognition technology]. As an example, effective two-factor authentication would require that when access is being requested, proof would be required from at least two different categories.

N is for Network Segmentation

nagware – a form of software that persistently reminds the user that he or she should do something, even though he or she might not want to. This is not usually considered to be malicious software, but it does exhibit some unwanted features that disrupt the flow of the user's interaction with his or her **device**. Nagware is often used as partial payment for some forms of software, especially free software.

nanotechnology – incredibly small products and **devices** manufactured through the manipulation of items as small as atoms and molecules.

NAS – acronym for **N**etwork-**A**ttached **S**torage. A digital repository where information can be stored, that is attached to a **network**.

NAT – acronym for **N**etwork **A**ddress **T**ranslation. This is a **router protocol**, typically used in **firewalls** and other **devices**, to change (translate) the **IP address** between **network** addresses inside and outside a network **gateway**.

National Initiative for Cybersecurity Education (NICE) – a US government initiative to help enhance the training and resources for the defense of digital technologies and the electronic information they contain and transact.

network – a collective group of **devices**, wiring and **applications** used to connect, carry, broadcast, monitor or safeguard **data**. Networks can be physical (use material **assets** such as wiring) or virtual (use applications to create associations and connections between devices or applications). Usually, the devices on a network will have some form of trusted permissions that allow them to pass and share **packets** of electronic information.

network-based – describes a situation where something is installed to protect, serve or subvert the community of **devices**, wiring and **applications** used to connect, carry, broadcast, monitor or safeguard information (the **network**).

Network-based Intrusion Prevention Systems (NIPS) – see

Intrusion Prevention Systems.

network forensics – a part of the **digital forensics** discipline, focused on investigating and uncovering evidence. This includes rebuilding and recovering electronic information from the **device**s used to connect and carry information between **endpoints**. Advances in defensive technology can now allow (for example) all communicated **data** packages to be captured for a period of time. When this technology is in place, even if the sending and receiving endpoint devices are initially unknown, information about what took place can still be acquired because the incoming and outgoing data packages that were transmitted can be replayed in full. See also **indicators of compromise**.

network interface controller (NIC) – the component within any **digital device** that enables it to communicate with other digital devices running a similar component.

network protection – the defensive and protective measures taken to secure a specific set of interconnected **device**s. **Firewalls** are an example of a **network** protection technology.

network recording – a form of **cyber defense** that allows an organization to store a copy of all inbound and outbound **data** transmissions for a period of time. After any **cyber incident**, this allows the **incident response** team to review what data may have been compromised and to also apply **digital forensics** to help identify the perpetrators.

network security – the defensive and protective measures taken to protect a specific set of interconnected **devices**. **Firewalls** are an example of a network security technology.

network segmentation – splitting a single collection of **devices**, wiring and **applications** that connect, carry, broadcast, monitor or safeguard **data** into smaller sections. This allows for more discrete management of each section, allowing greater security to be applied in sections with the highest value, and also permitting smaller sections to be impacted in the event of a **malware** infection or other disruptive event. This is one **method** of a security technique known as **compartmentalization**.

network sniffer – see **sniffing**.

network traffic analysis – the act of recording, reviewing and inspecting key information about the **data** that is transacted over **digital devices** and infrastructure used to connect and transport electronic information. This technique is used extensively by **Intrusion Detection and Prevention Systems** and other **network security** sensors. The information collected can also be used toward advanced threat detection and **digital forensics** as an **indicator of compromise**.

NFC – acronym for **N**ear **F**ield **C**ommunication. A **method** of extremely short-range **data** communication that uses electromagnetic induction and usually operates by touching contiguous NFC-enabled **device**s or by targeting devices that are a maximum of 2 inches, or 5 cm, away.

NIC – see **network interface controller**.

NICE – see **National Initiative for Cybersecurity Education**.

NIST – acronym for the US **N**ational **I**nstitute of **S**tandards & **T**echnology.

NOC – acronym for **N**etwork **O**perations **C**enter, traditionally the place from which the real-time security of major computer **network**s would be monitored and managed.

node – a place in any **network** where the pathway branches, meets or otherwise intersects another pathway.

non-repudiation – the act of ensuring that a user's electronic activity has sufficient identity checks and **audit** evidence in place so that it cannot be refuted or denied by the person performing the action.

noob – a person that is new to a particular field or environment and an indication that he or she may be more vulnerable to being targeted. The term is believed to derive from the colloquial term *newbie* blended with the term *roob* (or *rube*), meaning someone unsophisticated, unintelligent or of low capability.

NotPetya – a notable piece of **malware** (malicious software) that began to spread in late June 2017. This **cyber attack** spread initially via an update system of a financial software company popular in the Ukraine. Just like the **WannaCry** attack that had spread the month before, the malware contained a large number of rogue tactics including the **exploit** known as **Eternal Blue**. The infection rate rapidly impacted enterprises and **devices** that had not implemented recent software updates and that also had weak security configurations. Although the software was designed to initially look like **ransomware**, it turned out to be a **wiper** – software designed to completely delete the contents of devices it infects. The recovery costs involved for the enterprises that were impacted by this attack have been estimated to be upwards of $4 billion. Due to the initial target **vector** and subsequent analysis of the code, the US and UK have attributed this attack to Russia. See also **attribution** and **cyber false flag**.

O is for OWASP

Oauth – a portmanteau of *Open authentication*, the name given to an **Internet Protocol** that can enable **application**s to have access different from and greater than the user who is accessing it, so that the application can perform tasks requiring such additional permissions.

open source – an **application**, other computer program or software building block for which the software code is made publicly available for expansion, use or modification by anybody. This makes it very cheap to use, but also opens up a greater potential for malicious subversion, especially if subverted versions of the work are incorporated into **systems** that are intended to be secure.

openSSL – an **open source** version of the Secure Sockets Layer **protocol** used to help provide **authentication** and **cryptographic** security between two parties. This protocol is used widely on Internet **web servers** and websites to help prevent interception, intrusion and falsification as communications are passed between a legitimate host and the intended recipient of the **data**.

Open Web Application Security Project – see **OWASP**.

operating system – the central, low-level software **application** program in any **digital device** that enables the hardware (screen, buttons, etc) to interact with any installed software.

orchestration – in the context of **cybersecurity**, this is the process of collecting, analyzing, coordinating and controlling information (**policies**, logs, instructions, …) across technologies and processes used to sustain security. As **devices**, information and technologies are increasingly subject to **containerization**, orchestration helps to sustain a coordinated view across a segmented **digital landscape**.

out-of-band – in the context of **cybersecurity**, this is where a security filter or technology performs its analysis and decision making away from the filters or **controls** it can operate, to prevent or block an **attack**. Instead of traffic passing directly through the security **device** (**in-line**), information about the traffic is sent to a separate control location. Although the response time for out-of-band security is slower, this technique allows for more comprehensive and consistent coordination of security in very large environments.

OWASP – the **O**pen **W**eb **A**pplication **S**ecurity **P**roject is an online community that aims to create free, public resources to help improve the security of software. For example, it maintains lists of the leading **vulnerabilities** and security **controls**.

P is for Patch Management

PaaS – acronym meaning **P**latform **a**s **a S**ervice. **Applications** are developed and deployed on **platform**s. This type of **cloud** service allows the development and deployment of new applications to take place for a lower cost and with faster scalability than setting up the equivalent in a private **network** would allow. The cost benefits and scalability are achieved through the use of shared infrastructure and pre-configured virtual machines. When the platform is public (open to the Internet) and needs to be secure, additional security is required, compared to a private platform, to achieve the equivalent perimeter protection. See also **cloud**.

packet – (in the context of electronic communication) is a bundle of electronic information grouped together for transmission. The bundle usually includes **control information** to indicate the destination, source and type of content, and the content (user information) itself.

packet-filtering – passing or blocking bundles of electronic information inbound or outbound based on specific rules. For example, if a known **threat** uses a particular size, format and type of **data** package (**packet**), then a rule can be put in place, on either an advanced **firewall** or a similar **device**, to block content that matches those parameters from leaving or entering a **network**. See also **packet**. Also known as **content filtering**.

packet replay – to repeat a sequence of **data** bundles that have been previously captured or recorded. As an example of usage, this technique can be used after **network** traffic has been recorded to review which bundles of information were transacted during an **attack**.

packet sniffer – see **sniffing**.

password – a secret string of characters (letters, numbers and other special characters) that can be used to gain entry to a **digital device**, **application** or other service.

password salting – see **salting**.

patch management – a controlled process used to deploy critical, interim updates to software on **digital devices**. The release of a software 'patch' is usually in response to a critical flaw or gap that has been identified. Any failure to apply new interim software updates promptly can leave open security **vulnerabilities** in place. As a consequence, promptly applying these updates (patch management) is considered a critical component of maintaining effective **cybersecurity**.

payload – the part of the **data** in a transmission that constitutes the usable content (the cargo) rather than the packaging (the header or routing information). In the context of **cybersecurity**, this term is often used to refer to the harmful data (**malware**, for example) that an **attacker** may attempt to send into a target **digital device**, **network**, or **system**. For example, an attacker **exploits** a **vulnerability** to deliver his or her payload of malware.

payload analysis – the recording, review and study of the primary **data** content (electronic information) contained in **network** transmission **packets**. This can be used to detect any unexpected, unauthorized or unwelcome incoming or outgoing information transactions; for example, to help detect or prevent **malware** from entering a network, or to help detect or prevent confidential information from leaving a network. This can also be used as an **indicator of compromise**.

peer-to-peer – the ability to make a transaction between two **digital devices** (computers) without the need for a central server.

penetration – (in the context of **cybersecurity**) – intrusion.

penetration test (also known as an **attack and penetration test** or **pen. test**) – checks and scans on any **application**, **system** or website to identify any potential security gaps (**vulnerabilities**) that could be **exploited**. It is a form of **dynamic testing**. Once the vulnerabilities are identified, this process then goes on to identify the extent to which these vulnerabilities could be leveraged in an **attack** (the penetration possibilities). Usually these checks are performed in a test area and emulate the same techniques that could be used by an **attacker**. This is to prevent any inadvertent operational disruption. The checks are typically conducted before any application or site is first used, and also on a periodic (repeating) basis; for example, each time the program is updated or every 6 months. Any significant gaps must be addressed (fixed) in a timeframe appropriate to the scale of the **risk**. Not to be confused with the term **vulnerability assessment**, which only identifies gaps without examining how they could be leveraged. See also **pivoting**.

penetration tester – a person who performs simulated attempts at **attack** on a target **system** or **application** on behalf of the organization that owns or **controls** it. See also **penetration test**

and **pivoting**.

pen. test – see **penetration test**.

periscope up – when people hold a **smart device** up at head level or higher to capture an event on the device's camera.

persistence – to seek continued existence despite opposition.

persistent (non-reflective) cross-site scripting – a more devastating form of web **vulnerability** that can impact large numbers of users due to security gaps in the design of some web **applications**. Unwanted and unexpected code (programs) can be pushed to an application server by an **attacker**. When a legitimate user accesses the compromised web application, the attacker's **script** (mini program or link) can then be run automatically without any further user action. This is generally considered a critical **risk** category because it can target all users of an application. See also **reflective (non-persistent) cross-site scripting**.

personally identifiable information (**PII**) – any combination of information that can directly or indirectly distinguish (identify) who a specific individual is.

phantom vibration – when you think you felt your **smart device** vibrate but find out that it did not, or when you realize that there is no smart device on that area of your body right now.

pharming – a form of **cyber attack** in which the traffic intended for a particular web page or website is redirected to another location under the control of the attacker. The attacker may then steal information that the victim believes is going to the legitimate site, or use the connection to the page to infiltrate the computing device of the target. This usually requires some degree of infiltration of either the website itself or the **DNS**

service it uses.

phishing – using a communication (for example email, physical letter or instant messaging) that pretends to come from a legitimate source, in an attempt to get sensitive information (for example, a **password** or credit card number) from the recipient or to install **malware** on the recipient's **device**. The **method**s of phishing through electronic communications have evolved so that the message can simply contain a link to an Internet location where malware is situated or can include an attachment (such as a PDF or Word document) that installs malware when opened. The malware can then be used to run any number of unauthorized functions, including stealing information from the device, replicating additional malware to other accessible locations, sharing the user screen and logging keyboard entries made by the user. Less complex forms of phishing can encourage the recipient to visit a fake but convincing version of a website, or call a telephone number where they may then persuaded to disclose passwords or other details.

physical security – measures designed to deter, prevent, detect or alert unauthorized real-world access to a site or material item.

piggybacking – (in the context of **cybersecurity**) – the act of using a legitimate activity or data exchange to insert or add other actions. This can refer to the illicit use of a **network** or Internet connection belonging to someone else (to piggyback a connection). It can also refer to the addition of content within a web page so that when a person loads in the expected content, they also load in additional components from one or more third parties that has been placed in the same page, often with the consent of the webpage owner – a technique used in **pixel tracking**. The same term is also sometimes used as an alternative to **tailgating**, in which an intruder attempts to physically follow an authorized person through a controlled access point (such as a locked door) in close enough proximity so that the lock does not have time to re-engage.

PII – see **personally identifiable information**.

PIN – acronym for **P**ersonal **I**dentification **N**umber. Originally a short sequence of numbers that could be used as part of an **authentication** or **authorization** process, especially for ATMs and simple door access keypads. Some PINs may now include non-numeric characters. A PIN is effectively a type of **password**, but the term is usually applied either when the PIN is required in addition to a password, and/or to indicate to the end user that a smaller set of potential character options (such as numbers only) is available. It is worth noting that the use of a PIN with a password is not considered to be a form of **multi-factor authentication,** but is an example of using two forms of a single-factor authentication (in this example, the single factor is *something you know*). See also **multi-factor authentication**.

pivot – (1) a **method** used by **penetration testers** and **attackers** to leverage a point of infiltration as a route for easier access to compromise, infect and/or **attack** other **systems** and **networks**. (2) to use a piece of information during a **malware** investigation as a source for pattern analysis to help reveal information about an **incident** and how to resolve it.

pixel tracking – a technique that allows a website owner and advertisers or **hackers** that buy tiny image files called pixels on the website to acquire information about the **digital devices** that visit the site. The technique can also be used in emails. A pixel consists of a 1 x 1 square on a screen. Modern image resolutions mean there are usually hundreds of pixels per square inch of computer screen. The computer code in a pixel causes **cookies** to be placed on digital devices when their users visit the site. The cookies allow the presence of a pixel to be used to deliver targeted advertising and to remember specific users and their online activities when they visit again. Pixel tracking also allows information about users to be immediately sent to the tracker's server so it is not lost if a user deletes the cookies on his or her machine. Information about device type, page visits and other details can therefore still be aggregated over time. Pixel tracking has been a common practice for many technology **platform**s for a long time, with many popular web pages selling pixel tracking space to large numbers of third parties. This is part of the reason that many email services ask for permission before any images are displayed. Pixel tracking allows cookie information to be collected across a greater range of activities and page visits because it allows a large number of parties to have a very small interest in each web page.

PKI – see **public key infrastructure**.

platform (in the context of computing) – the combination of **hardware**, **operating system** and any other components required by a piece of **software** before it can run. For example, a **smart device** that relies on a sensor that is not present cannot run because its platform is incomplete.

playback attack – an alternative term for a **replay attack**. See **replay attack**.

policy – (i) a high-level statement of intent, often a short document, that provides guidance on the principles an organization follows. For example, a basic security policy document could describe the intention for an enterprise to ensure that all locations (physical and electronic) where information for which they are accountable must remain secure from any **unauthorized access**. A policy does not usually describe the explicit mechanisms or specific instructions that would be used to achieve or enforce the intentions it expresses; this would be described in a **procedure**. (ii) Alternatively, it can also be used to mean the settings (including security settings) inside a **software program** or **operating system**.

polymorphic malware – malicious software that can change its attributes to help avoid detection by **anti-malware**. This mutation process can be automated so that the function of the software continues, but the method of operation, location and other attributes may change. See also **metamorphic malware** and **blended threat**.

pop a shell – the act of breaking into the **operating system** or command-level **control** system (**shell**) of a computing **device**.

port – a connection point (real or virtual) that helps in the transmission of electronic **data** between electronic **devices** and computer programs. Assigning a specific value (a **port number**) when sending information lets the receiver know what type of information is being sent and how it should be processed. This information can also be used by security devices such as **firewalls** to help allow or deny certain communication types.

port number – used as part of an electronic communication to denote the **method** of communication being used. This allows the **packet** to be directed to a program that will know what to do with it.

port scanning – a process, usually run by computer, to detect open access points (**port**s) that could be used to infiltrate or **exfiltrate** electronic information into or out of an enterprise.

pretexting – a form of **social engineering** in which the **attacker** pretends to have a fake situation, usually involving time pressure and emotional duress, in order to get the victim to perform a task he or she would usually refuse to do. For example, the attacker may pretend to be in the middle of an emergency to pressure the victim into bypassing his or her normal identity or **authorization** checks.

preventive control – (see also **control**) a **method** of security defense used to stop issues before they can become problematic. For example, **multi-factor authentication** assists in stopping

unauthorized access from ever occurring and is therefore considered a preventive control.

private cloud – see **cloud computing**.

private key – a unique **encryption device** or formula provided to a specific individual or specific service as one part of an encryption **system**. See **asymmetric cryptography**.

private virtual address space – an area of computer **memory** designed to keep electronic information isolated (secure and secret) from other processes, without the need for that **data** to take-up real memory space during use by a computer.

privileged account – an electronic user **access right** that has elevated permissions to allow it to perform **system**, **application**, database or other **digital landscape** management functions. Usually, this form of access requires additional **controls** and supervision to ensure the elevated privileges are fully accountable and are not misused. Most forms of **cyber attack** seek to gain this form of access, as these types of accounts have control over their digital landscape.

privileged account management – the **systems**, technologies and processes used to monitor and **control** the activities of **privileged accounts**.

privilege escalation – this is a technique used in the majority of **cyber attack**s in which the **hacker** seeks to raise his or her **access rights** to an **administrator access** level. This expands the footprint and **control** permissions that the **attacker** has across the **digital landscape** he or she is targeting.

procedure – provides guidance or specific instruction on the process (**method**) that should be used to achieve an objective. Traditionally provided as a document available to appropriate personnel, but increasingly replaced by instructions that are built into computer **systems** to enforce the required steps. In a traditional quality model, procedures may reside under a **policy** as an explicit instruction for meeting a particular policy objective. See also **policy** definition (i).

procedural control – an instruction during a sequence of required steps to limit how something is or is not permitted to be used.

processor – the part of any computer that executes the real-time instructions and calculations. Modern **devices** usually have many different processors so that larger numbers of instructions can be executed in synchrony. Processors may also be dedicated to particular types of instructions; for example, a GPU is a Graphics Processing Unit that is usually used to process image rendering, whereas a CPU is a Central Processing Unit used to run general tasks. See also **Moore's Law**.

promiscuous mode – a setting for a **network interface controller** that allows it to pass all information it receives for inspection; usually used when **packet sniffing** is in operation.

protected memory – any part of the active storage in a **digital device** that is protected either by hardware or software so that it does not share information with unauthorized processes. Protected memory often makes use of **private virtual address space**. See also **Spectre** for a **memory exploit** example.

protection from detection – to distill information about upgraded security processes or technology requirements based on intelligence and analysis of security issues and **incident**s. A reactive security approach.

protocol – (in the context of electronic communications) is a set of established rules used to send information between different electronic locations. Protocols provide a standard that can be used to send or receive information in an expected and understandable format, including information about the source, destination and route. Examples of protocols include **Internet protocol (IP)**, **hyper text transfer protocol (HTTP)**, **file transfer protocol (FTP)**, **transmission control protocol (TCP)**, **border gateway protocol (BGP)** and **dynamic host configuration protocol (DHCP)**.

proxy server – is a program used to provide intermediate services between a requested transaction and its destination. Instead of sending the transaction 'as is' it can adjust some of the information to help secure the anonymity of the sender. In addition, it may store (**cache**) any information that is accessed often to help speed up response times.

psychographics – a form of advanced demographics that can be used to target or influence people based not only on their geographic location but also on deeper personal information such as their age, income, interests, beliefs, friendships, traits, values, attitudes, opinions, lifestyle, etc. See also **behavioral microtargeting**.

PsyOps – a portmanteau of **Psy**chological **Op**erations. The tactical use of an understanding of the human mind (psychology) to change, persuade or influence a person's actions.

public – (in the context of **cybersecurity**) indicates that the artifact used in any prefix or suffix is openly available and accessible over the Internet.

public cloud – a low-cost, multi-tenant environment in which computing resources are rapidly shared and re-provisioned across many different customers using virtualization technology. A public cloud environment offers rapidly scalable, pay-as-you-go computing at a scale and cost that private firms can usually not achieve on their own. See also **virtual machine** and **hypervisor**.

public key cryptography – see **asymmetric cryptography**.

public key encryption – see **asymmetric cryptography**.

public key infrastructure (PKI) – the set of hardware, **applications** and processes needed to manage **public key encryption**.

PUPs – acronym for **P**otentially **U**nwanted **P**rograms. Describes a type of software that the user may have **consent**ed to download but that performs some undesirable or potentially malicious functions. Often, this kind of software may be bundled in with other software that the user has consented to download.

PuTTY – a text-oriented **terminal emulator** that can be used to put raw commands and other instructions, including file transfers, directly into digital components such as **SSH** and **command line interface**s.

pwned – domination or humiliation of a rival, originating from video game play but also applied to **cybersecurity attacks**.

Q is for Quarantine

quantum computing – a new generation of computers capable of a step change in processing speed for many calculation types that is hundreds of millions times faster than current computer technology. Early versions have already been developed for use but are not expected to reach their true potential until around 2025; however, this date seems pessimistic based on current progress. Quantum computers replace binary (0 and 1) information storage and processing with exponentially better techniques involving multi-dimensional **data** handling using quantum physics. For example, the *bits* in traditional computers can only handle being in a state of 1 or 0. The **qubits** in a quantum computer make use of quantum physics to be able to store, 0, 1 or a superposition of both states. Unlike traditional computers in which the increase in bits causes a linear increase in **memory** capacity, an increasing number of *qubits* in which the principles of quantum entanglement can be leveraged creates an exponential growth in capacity. A stable quantum computer with 300 qubits can theoretically store more pieces of information than there are atoms in the Universe. This technology, once stable and mature, will be able to defeat any mathematically based **encryption** within minutes. This means that technology experts expect traditional (math-based) encryption to be defunct and replaced by **quantum encryption** within the next 10 to 12 years.

quantum cryptography – the encoding and decoding of information to the extent that the **cipher** techniques will not be easy for **quantum computer**s to **crack**. See **quantum computing** and **quantum encryption**.

quantum encryption – a method of **cipher**ing or hiding information using physics rather than mathematics. For example, using atomic attributes such as spinning a photon in a particular way, it is possible to encode information so that any incorrect attempt to decipher it will render it permanently unreadable. This kind of technique can also be used to create content that can only be deciphered at a given point in time. Quantum encryption makes use of quantum computing, however, information using quantum cryptography may also refer to any method designed to have features that quantum computers cannot easily crack.

quarantine – the act of isolating any known or suspected **malware** so that it can do no further damage to digital information and **assets**, usually as a precursor to removal or examination. See also **containment**.

qubits – a portmanteau of **qu**antum **bit**, also sometimes referred to as a qbit. This is a term used to represent a single unit of quantum information that is one of the building blocks inside **quantum computing**. See **quantum computing**.

quidproquo – the **social engineering** technique of offering a victim something of perceived value (where the value may be real or not) in return for an action or gift from the victim. The action can be as simple as clicking on a link, adjusting a control in a computing **device** or a gift such as making a financial payment. The action or gift by the victim is subsequently either misused and/or proven to have been elicited under false pretences.

R is for Rainbow Tables

rainbow tables – a set of precomputed **encryption** values that can be used to reverse engineer items such as hash values back to their unencrypted value. These can be used to help **crack** (reveal) an encrypted value. As an example, most short hash values that use standard hash techniques can be entered into Google to reveal their unencrypted value.

RAM – acronym for **R**andom **A**ccess **M**emory. The part of any computer or **digital device** in which information is stored for active use by the **processor**. Unlike a hard disk or some other forms of **memory**, the information in standard RAM is only retained when the device it belongs to has power. If power to the RAM is lost, the contents of the RAM will no longer be present.

ransomware – a form of malicious software (**malware**) that prevents or restricts usage of one or more **digital devices** or

applications or renders a collection of electronic **data** unreadable until a sum of money is paid. **Cryptoviral extortion** is an example of the techniques used to perform this type of **attack**.

RASP – acronym for **R**eal-time **A**pplication **S**ecurity **P**rotection. An advanced form of checking software for deficiencies and vulnerabilities in live (production) environments, with additional features that can then automatically alert and defend against the actions of an attacker. As with interactive application security testing (**IAST**), this is achieved by deploying small programs (agents) within and around the application components. RASP is effectively similar to IAST but with additional functionality to go beyond detecting security deficiencies to include detecting and responding to suspected attacks. See also **IAST** and **DevSecOps**.

RAT – a remote access tool or remote access **trojan** that is used as a form or component of **malware** to help **attackers** gain **control** over a target computer or other **digital device**.

RDP – acronym for **R**emote **D**esktop **P**rotocol, a graphical interface that allows a user to access the desktop of another computer. This can be useful for administration of multiple computers from a single device but **vulnerabilities** in configuration or deployment can be targeted by **cyber criminals** and other **threat actors**.

recovery point objective (**RPO**) – the maximum amount of **data** loss or **corrupt**ion that can be permitted (often expressed as an amount of time) in the event of a **system** disruption. This in turn sets the **backup** and other failsafe requirements for a system. For example, a hotel or airline flight booking system may have a zero tolerance for any data loss (no transactions can be permitted to be lost – because they cannot be recovered through any other means), which requires that the system has an infallible **method** of logging all transactions so they can always be recovered. Note: This is a different parameter than system **availability**, as it only covers whether (and how much) entered data can be lost to the owner. For availability – see **recovery time objective (RTO)**.

recovery time objective (RTO) – the targeted number of days, hours, minutes or seconds within which a service, **application** or process must be restored, if it is subject to disruption. This should be based on the **availability** rating set by the owner (the recovery time objective must not exceed the availability requirement).

red team – when testing for potential **exploits** affecting any critical or sensitive **system**, infrastructure or website, a team of **penetration testers** is usually used. This term is used to describe the group of penetration testers working together on this type of objective.

reflective (non-persistent) cross-site scripting – a form of web **vulnerability** that can impact individual users due to security gaps in the design of some web **applications**. Unwanted and unexpected code (programs) can be run on a user's machine if the individual can be persuaded to click on or interact with content that may look legitimate, but is in fact a link to **malware**. This is generally considered a lower **risk** category than **persistent (non-reflective) cross-site scripting** because it can only target individual users (not the host application) and requires considerable effort for low return from **hackers**, plus additional user action. See also **persistent (non-reflective) cross-site scripting**.

registry – the low-level settings and options in an **operating system** that tell a **digital device** about items such as the hardware and basic security configuration options that have been selected in the configuration files. Compromising or changing these settings can be used for various types of **cyber attacks**.

replay attack – a **method** of stealing a copy of information and re-sending it to perform fraudulent transactions. For example, an **attacker** might steal a message sent from a company executive to the company's financial disbursement officer, requesting a money transfer. Later, this attacker re-sends the message in its original form to the same recipient, who will probably not be suspicious because the message matches the legitimate one that was previously sent. Or, an attacker might record a **password** when it is used to authorize a transaction, and may then use the password to perform further transactions. However, this form of **attack** usually targets more sophisticated challenge/response information than password information. **Man-in-the-middle** is an example of a replay attack.

residual risk – refers to the remaining possibility of loss and impact after security **controls** (the **risk** response) for an item have been applied.

resilience – the ability to remain functional and capable in the face of **threat** or danger, or to return to function rapidly following any disruption.

response management – see **incident response**.

risk – a situation involving exposure to significant impact or loss. In formal frameworks, risk can be quantified using probability (often expressed as a percentage) and impact (often expressed as a financial amount). Other parameters for risk can include proximity (how soon a potential risk may be encountered), and information about which **assets**, services, products and processes could be affected.

risk assessment – a systematic process for the proactive detection of potential hazards or gaps in an existing or planned activity, **asset**, service, **application**, **system** or product.

risk-based – an approach that considers the financial impact of a failure, along with its probability and proximity, to determine its comparative significance and priority for treatment.

risk register – a central repository that contains entries for each potential, significant loss or damage exposure. Usually, there is a minimum **materiality** threshold; for example, a minimum potential financial loss value that must be met or exceeded before an entry in the repository is required. If a **risk** does occur, it technically becomes an issue (rather than a risk). Items can continue to be tracked within a risk register until the impact has been successfully managed and the root cause(s) have been resolved to the extent that the risk is not likely to occur again.

rogueware – see **scareware**.

rootkit – a set of software tools that can be used by **attackers** to gain privileged access and **control** of the core (root) of the target **device**, where commands can be more easily run than if attackers fail to gain **administrative access**. Part of the function of a rootkit usually includes hiding malicious files and processes to help avoid detection and removal of the **malware**.

router – a **device** used to define the path for **data packets** (electronic information) to follow when they flow between **networks**.

runtime – the length of time for which a software **application** operates.

S is for Steganography

SaaS – acronym for **S**oftware **a**s **a S**ervice – a type of **cloud** service in which **applications** or other software are hosted online by a cloud server rather than being physically owned, stored or managed by the customer who uses the software. This reduces the cost and adds on-demand scalability. See also **cloud (the)**.

salting – is a security concealment process often applied to **password** storage security. When a user selects a password, it usually needs to be a relatively short string of characters and numbers and may not be unique (other users may have selected the same password). The password is usually concealed using a process known as **hashing**. Salting is the process of adding a long, unique and random string of characters to the password before it is subject to hashing. This is to ensure that (for example) if two users choose the same password, the hash value will still be different because the value represents the combination of the password and the unique random information. Salting also helps to reduce the possibility of being able to perform a reverse lookup of the 'hash' value to uncover the password through search engines and **rainbow tables**.

sandboxing – a **method** used by some **anti-malware** solutions to temporarily place content in a safe area (usually for a matter of seconds) to observe its behavior before allowing it into the real **domain**. This is used to help identify **malware** when coupled with traditional **signature** techniques. Some advanced malware is now written to account for this technique, and includes a time delay before it exhibits any rogue behavior, thereby circumventing this defensive technique.

scareware – malicious software that is designed to persuade people to buy an antidote for a computer infection. It usually masquerades as a commercial **malware** removal tool or **anti-virus** package, but in reality is provided by the **attacker**.

script – one or more technical instructions, written in a programming language, that can be used to tell a remote computer how to perform one or more specified tasks. This can be used, for example, within a web page so that a mini program (script) within the page can verify that the entry of an email address uses the right format without the need to send the information back to the web server. The script is run on the local computer but was sent to that local computer from the web server.

script bunny – see **script kiddies**.

script kiddies – **attacker**s with little to no coding (programming) or technical skills who make use of available **script**s, codes and packages to gain **unauthorized access** to **digital devices, applications, systems** and/or **networks**. Also known as **script bunnies** and **skiddies**.

secure configuration – ensuring that when settings are applied to any item (**device** or software), appropriate steps are always taken to ensure (i) **default accounts** are removed or disabled, (ii) shared accounts are not used and (iii) all protective and defensive **controls** in the item use the strongest appropriate setting(s).

secure file transfer protocol (also known as **SFTP**) – see **file transfer protocol** (**FTP**).

secure hyper text transfer protocol (**SHTTP**) – see **hyper text transfer protocol**.

security analytics – the collation of log file and record information from technologies and processes designed to detect and defend a **digital landscape**, for the purpose of reviewing and defining any significant patterns, trends or gaps in the security posture.

security architecture – a model designed to specify the features and **controls** across a **digital landscape** that help it to prevent, detect and control any attempts at disruption or **unauthorized access**. The model also ensures that all **data** exchanges are subject to appropriate standards sufficient to ensure that the **data controller'**s **chain of custody** commitments are maintained.

security by design – the embedding of protective and defensive measures into the lifecycle of any **digital device** or service from the earliest stage of requirements planning.

security event – a term used to describe a minor disruption to the **digital landscape** that is thought to be unintentional. Examples include a single failed **device** or a single user forgetting his or her **password**. Unusual patterns of security events can be an indicator of a **security incident**.

security gateways – this term is used to describe the collection of protection **method**s used at the edge of devices, across their communication channels, on the perimeter of applications and at boundaries between **networks** and **network segments**. As the protection of **digital devices** has evolved, the defensive options for the edge of devices and their communication channels have also increased in number. Within an enterprise, these gateway protection methods are usually defined in a **security architecture** that would not only look at which **firewalls** are in place at the edge of a network, but more broadly would inspect the specifications for all of the **security gateways** placed on internal communication channels, devices and other assets within the network. This could include the **VPN**, **IDPS**, software firewalls and other security gateway technologies.

security incident – the intentional damage, theft and/or **unauthorized access** that has direct or indirect impact to any substantial part of an organization's information, **systems**, **devices**, services or products.

Security Incident & Event Management – see **SIEM**.

security incident responder – a person who assists in the initial analysis and response to any known or suspected attempt at damage, interruption or **unauthorized access** to an organization's **information systems** or services.

security misconfiguration – one of the **OWASP** top 10 critical security flaws to guard against. To fail to adequately apply security settings or up-to-date security patches to any component in a **digital landscape** or specific **software program**.

Security Operations Center – see the entry for **SOC**.

security testing and monitoring – an umbrella reference used to encompass all of the technologies and processes used to verify that appropriate protection and defensive measures are in place. **Static source code testing**, **penetration testing**, **vulnerability scanning** and **file integrity monitoring** are some examples of security testing and monitoring activities.

self-healing networks – a collection of **digital devices** that have a certain level of trust and interconnectivity in which connections can be established or broken on an ad-hoc basis to overcome operational and security issues. To successfully make and break these connections requires some level of **machine learning** or **artificial intelligence** to help assure connections are only made or broken for appropriate reasons.

Senders Policy Framework (SPF) – see **SPF**.

sensitive data exposure – one of the **OWASP** top 10 critical security flaws to guard against. This flaw results from a failure to implement adequate measures to protect high-value information within a software **application** or web page. When a software application or web page transacts information of high value (for example, credit card **data**, health information or even **password**s), extra security measures should be in place to protect it from being read or intercepted by unauthorized parties. This usually requires using techniques for **encryption** when the data is at rest (stored) or in-transit (communicated between points). It also requires protecting data that is **in-memory** (being actively processed). This flaw can also result from other security gaps such as **using components with known vulnerabilities**.

session management – when a person or digital service interacts to and fro with another piece of software or web-based service without interruption, the transactions are considered to be part of one related set of activities between the two parties (a session). To retain continuity and avoid the need for repeated **authentication**, software has to adequately recognize when activities are part of an existing session, or when an activity is part of a new session, requiring new authentication. The process of managing these interactions without the need for re-authentication is known as session management.

sextortion – the technique of pretending to have compromising, explicit images or footage of the victim that will be released to their contacts or uploaded to a public Internet location unless the victim agrees to pay a ransom. The images usually do not exist but the attacker will sometimes use other confidential information they have, for example, an old password from the user, in order to make the attack more convincing.

shadow IT – technology that is adopted by an organization without going through official **assessment** and approval to ensure the correct security is in place. See also **employee-led cloud adoption** and **BYOC**.

SHA1 – acronym for **S**ecure **H**ash **A**lgorithm **1**. This is a legacy **cryptographic** standard designed around 1995 that is no longer considered secure. It was followed by SHA-2 in 2001 and SHA-3 in 2015. A challenge with all forms of **encryption** is that their security tends to be time-based; encryption considered strong or undefeatable at one point in time becomes defeatable years later as computing power increases.

shell – the user interface within the **operating system** of any **digital device**. Most **cyber attackers** seek to gain access to the shell because it gives them a privileged level of access to the **devices** they are attempting to subvert. See also **pop-a-shell**.

shell access – command-level permission to perform executive **control** over an electronic **device**.

shellshock – is the name given to a family of security **bugs**, discovered in September 2014. These bugs can be used to **attack** certain **devices** that work on the Unix bash **shell platform** if they have not had appropriate up-to-date software **patch management** applied. Vulnerable (unpatched) **systems** can be compromised to allow the **attacker** to gain **unauthorized access**. It was initially assigned the **CVE identifier** of CVE-2014-6271 but after this initial reporting, additional **vulnerabilities** were identified, and other CVE identifiers were assigned to the list of additional bugs. Also known as **bashdoor**.

shoulder surfing – the act of looking, unobserved, at the screen or keyboard of another person while he or she enters or reads information of value. The goal is to discover a **password**, obtain a credit card number or read a confidential email. The term reflects the fact that the optimum position for this intrusion is to stand behind the victim and read the content over his or her shoulder.

SIEM – abbreviation for **S**ecurity **I**ncident and **E**vent **M**anagement. This is a name given to the process and team that manages any form of minor or major interruption to an enterprise's **digital landscape**. See **incident response**.

signatures – (in the context of **cybersecurity**) are the unique attributes – for example, file size, file extension, **data** usage patterns and **method** of operation – that identify a specific computer program. Traditional **anti-malware** and other security technologies can make use of this information to identify and manage some forms of rogue software or communications.

single point (of) accountability (**SPA** or **SPOA**) – the principle that all critical **assets**, processes and actions must have clear ownership and traceability to a single person. The rationale is that the absence of a defined, single owner is a frequent cause of process or asset protection failure. Shared ownership is regarded as a significant security gap due to the consistent demonstration that security flaws have an increased probability of persisting when more than one person is accountable.

single point (of) failure – a **vulnerability** that is so significant, it can be used to create devastating disruption to an entire organization.

single-use malware – malicious software created for one-time use, in order to compromise a specific target. This type of **malware** has risen in popularity with **attackers** because it is relatively easy to produce and can evade many older forms of security software if they rely on **signatures** to identify **threats**.

singularity (**the**) – the predicted point in time when **artificial intelligence** exceeds human intelligence.

sinkhole – see **DNS sinkhole**.

skiddie – abbreviated form of **script kiddie**.

skimmer – a **device** attached to an ATM (UK term cashpoint) to steal (skim) a copy of information from a bank card as it is inserted into the cash machine. Such **device**s usually also include mechanisms to record the **PIN** that is entered either using a camera or a keyboard overlay.

skimming – stealing a copy of a layer of information from something. See also **digital skimming**.

smart (in the context of **digital devices** and **cybersecurity**) – a term used as a prefix to denote the addition of a small amount of controllable computer power inside an entity (e.g. *smartcity*) or object (e.g. *smartmeter*) to theoretically improve its performance. Although each *smart* technology has benefits, it also has disadvantages that usually include a much shorter lifespan than the items it replaces and weak security due to being built on the lowest possible budget to compete on mass-markets with non-smart versions of the same products. The security standards of smart technologies make them an ideal target for **threat actors**, especially for use as part of a **botnet** or **zombie army**. See also **Mirai**.

smishing – a **phishing attack** that uses the simple message service (**SMS**), to send a malicious link, file or other content (such as a contact phone number) to a phone as a text message. If the malicious link or attachment is opened the **device** may be compromised. If the number is contacted or replied to, it may carry premium rate charges and/or be used to elicit information from the victim. This form of attack can also use the **MMS** (multi-media service).

SMS – acronym for Short Message Service, the **protocol** used to send text messages between mobile phones. Longer messages use **MMS**. See also **MMS**.

sniffing (in the context of **cybersecurity**) – the act of monitoring and analyzing traffic to identify and resolve problems in a **network** (**network sniffer**), **data packet** (**packet sniffer**) or other level (for example, wireless sniffer).

Snort rules – the text (or code) that set how an open-source **IDS** (intrusion detection software) application (known as Snort) manages the information it processes to identify, detect, block or alert specific conditions.

SOC – acronym for **S**ecurity **O**perations **C**enter. A place where the real-time security situation for an enterprise is monitored and controlled. See also **SIEM**.

SOC automation – technologies that can help reduce the manual effort required to examine, resolve and escalate the information, events and **incident**s managed by a Security Operations Center (**SOC**). Due to the huge amount of **data** generated by modern security analysis technologies, the contents cannot be accurately filtered solely by manual efforts. As technologies improve, more and more analysis can be automated once security personnel choose an automated **platform** with tools that can be tailored to meet the organization's specific security needs. For example, *SOC automation* technologies can conduct real-time analysis of logs and can then automatically and immediately alert a suspicious trend in traffic. These technologies can also identify the user and files involved. Such an analysis would take a human operator weeks or months of investigation before he or she would notice any suspicious patterns.

social engineering – The act of constructing relationships, friendships or other human interactions for the purpose of enticing the recipient to perform an inadvisable action or reveal secret information. The individual(s) doing the social engineering use the victim's action or information for the hidden purpose of achieving a nefarious objective, such as acquiring intelligence about the security, location or **vulnerability** of **assets**, or even gaining the person's trust to open an Internet link or document that will result in a **malware** foothold being created.

software program – see **application**.

SPA – see **single point of accountability**.

spear phishing – a more targeted form of **phishing**. This term describes the use of an electronic communication (for example, email or instant messaging) that targets a particular person or group of people (for example, employees at a location) and pretends to come from a legitimate source. In this case, the source may also pretend to be someone known and trusted to the recipient, in an attempt to obtain sensitive information (for example, a **password** or credit card number).

Spectre – is a set of 2 security **vulnerabilities** revealed to the public in 2017, that requires chip manufacturers that use a process called *branch prediction* to adjust their **processor** design. In order to work as quickly as possible, many processors anticipate information that may be used and bring this into their local **cache** (side **memory**). As the Spectre vulnerabilities revealed, this process can leave the **data** open to potential observation or theft. The **CVE identifiers** issued for these vulnerabilities are CVE-2017-5753 and CVE-2017-5715. These vulnerabilities are notable because they have significantly impacted the future of processor design. The Spectre vulnerabilities also demonstrate that many legacy technologies have been built without **security by design** and that the fixes may result in decreased processor performance. The fact that the Spectre vulnerabilities were announced at the same time as the **Meltdown** vulnerability also made them notable.

SPF (in the context of **cybersecurity**) – acronym for **S**ender **P**olicy Framework – an email validation **system** to help prevent **spoofing** of messages by verifying that the **domain** from which an email claims to be is consistent with the value in a **Domain Name System (DNS)** record.

spoofing – concealing the true source of electronic information by impersonation or other means. Often used to bypass Internet security filters by pretending the source is from a trusted location, or by providing false information about the location of a source.

spyware – a form of **malware** that covertly gathers and transmits information from the **device** on which it is installed.

SQL injection – see **injection**.

SSH – acronym for **s**ecure **sh**ell – a **cryptographic protocol** for operating **network** instructions through a non-secure network.

SSID – acronym for **S**ervice **S**et **Id**entifier. This is the set of up to 32 characters that are used to recognize a particular Wireless Local Area Network (WLAN) connection on Wi-Fi **routers** and other access points. A list of the values can be seen when any **device** scans for visible wireless connections.

SSL – is an acronym for **S**ecure **S**ockets **L**ayer. This is a **method** (**protocol**) for providing **encrypted** communication between two points in a **digital landscape**. For example, this could be between a **web server** (the computer hosting a web service or website) and a **web browser** (the program that the recipient uses to view the webpage; for example, Internet Explorer). In the **URL** (the Internet address visible to the user), the use of SSL is denoted by an 'https:' prefix.

stacked risk – the phenomenon of allowing seemingly separate potential issues with potential impact (**risks**) affecting the same **digital landscape** to accumulate. Without adequate identification and resolution, individual risks can form a toxic accumulation of issues that can be leveraged together to create a risk substantially greater than the individual components suggest. **Megabreaches** are usually the result of stacked risk in combination with a motivated **attacker**.

stateful protocol analysis detection – is a **method** used by **intrusion detection systems** to identify malicious or unwanted communications. This method analyzes **packets** to determine if the source, destination, size and routing (**protocol**) is significantly different than its usual format.

static source code testing – see **static testing**.

static testing – (in the context of **cybersecurity**) to assess the security standards and potential **vulnerabilities** within the source code (program) of an **application**. This is a form of **white-box testing**. The use of the word *static* indicates that the item is not in an operational environment or active state when being tested – the components are being examined when they are at rest. Testing when an item is running or in the equivalent of an operational environment would instead be regarded as **dynamic testing**.

statistical anomaly-based detection – is a **method** used by some **intrusion detection systems** to identify malicious or unwanted communications. The program reviews the metrics it collects to identify any groups of communication behaviors that are unusual or anomalous.

steganalysis – the study of messages, image files and other objects to determine if and how they are carrying any concealed information. See also **steganography**.

steganography – to create or write concealed information of one type inside another message, image, file or other object so that only the sender and intended recipient know it is present. This is different than **encryption** because the information can still be in plain text; it is only the pattern or distribution used to conceal the information that may hide its presence. Derived from the Greek term for 'concealed writing.' This technique is used extensively in **cyber attacks** to move unwanted and otherwise unauthorized information in and out of secure locations, by disguising instructions and stolen **data** packages as standard communications. Steganography is often combined with encryption to make the covert communications even more difficult to identify and counteract. See also **image steganography**.

STIX – acronym for **S**tructured **T**hreat **I**nformation e**X**pression. Part of a language endeavoring to use standard structures and descriptors to help improve **data**-sharing about potential hostile actions and activities. This language includes the use of terms and structures defined in **CybOX** (cyber observables) and a communication architecture defined by **TAXII** (**T**rusted **A**utomated e**X**change of **I**ndicator **I**nformation).

structured query language injection (**SQL injection**) – a form of security **exploit** that takes advantage of security design flaws in web forms. Within some web pages, there are forms that users can complete. If a web form does not sufficiently validate (check) the content of the information returned to it, an **attacker** can create longer entries than expected that include commands that allow unauthorized and unexpected values into the database. The consequences can be the **corrupt**ion of the database and transactions.

stuxnet – a family of **malware** designed to target **control systems**, originally believed to have been designed to disrupt the Iranian nuclear program. This malware includes a **worm** and a **rootkit**. It has typically been delivered to target environments through the use of an infected **USB** stick (**jump drive**). There are multiple **CVE identifiers** associated with this **threat**.

sucker list – an identified set of soft targets that are easy to take advantage of due to their propensity to pay **ransomware** demands and/or to have a weak security position.

supercomputer – a **digital device** capable of performing calculations and other technical operations at a scale that is usually thousands of times greater than standard commercial digital devices of the time.

supply chain attack – the circumvention of in-house **cybersecurity controls** by an **attacker** through the use of a third party (such as a vendor) that has some degree of trusted access into the **systems** or technologies used by a target organization. The attacker can then use the trusted access of the third party as an infiltration point for malicious code insertion or other covert tactics.

surface web – the part of the **Internet** that is publically accessible and indexed by search engines.

swatting – a form of **social engineering** in which the **threat actor** makes a hoax call to intentionally provoke an armed response by security services to the address of their victim. The intended objective is the shooting of the victim.

symmetrical encryption – a **method** of changing plain text to and from secret (encoded) information using identical **key**s. In other words, the same key that is used to code the information into a secret format can be used to return the information to plain text. The **Advanced Encryption Standard** (**AES**) is an example of symmetrical encryption. See also **asymmetrical encryption**.

system administration – the configuration, maintenance and management functions in a **digital landscape**. This term can be applied to any **digital device**, electronic hardware, **system**, **network**, electronic service or **application**. This function requires the use of **privileged accounts**.

systems – groups of **applications** that operate together to serve a more complex purpose.

T is for Takedown

tailgating – following a person through a door or other physical access point at close enough proximity that any **method** intended to control the access is defeated. For example, if a door requires a code or pass to unlock it, the intruder aims to reach the door after someone legitimate has just used it and before the lock has had a chance to re-engage.

takedown – (i) the process of a defending organization rendering **malware** ineffective by removing its ability to perform its functions; for example, through **decapitation**. (ii) the process of an **attacker** making unavailable some or all of an organization's key **systems** or capabilities. (iii) to stop something from working.

TAXII – acronym for **T**rusted **A**utomated e**X**change of **I**ndicator **I**nformation. This is a standard used to define the communication architecture for **cyber threat intelligence** sharing. See **STIX** for further information.

technical control – the use of an electronic or digital **method** to influence or command how something like a **digital device** can or cannot be used. For example, removing the ability to cut or paste information in a smartphone is an example of a technical control that can be used to minimize security **risks**.

Technical Disaster Recovery Plan – an operational document that describes the exact process, people, information and **assets** required to put any electronic or digital **system** back in place within a timeline defined by the **business continuity plan**. If there are multiple business continuity plans that reference the same Technical Disaster Recovery Plan, the restoration time used must meet the shortest time specified in any of the documents.

Telnet – a text-oriented command interface and **protocol** that can be used to send instructions to another **device** that is connected on the same **network**. By leveraging unexpected, unguarded or unofficial connections, this **method** can be used as part of a **cyber attack**.

terminal emulator – ("tty" for short) is a **software program**

that provides a visual window that acts as a **method** of providing text-based command line or other instructions to a target **device**.

thin client – in software architecture, the **endpoint** where a user interacts with a **software program** is known as a *client*. When a software program requires little or no local installation (for example, if it works via a standard **web browser**), it is regarded as having little to no footprint or **processor** usage and is considered to have a *thin client*. See also **fat client**.

threat – any source of potential harm to the **digital landscape**.

threat actors – an umbrella term to describe the collection of people and organizations that work to create **cyber attacks**. Examples of threat actors include **cyber criminals**, **hacktivists** and nation states.

threat intelligence – the collation of information about potential hostile actions that could occur, together with an understanding of their relative probabilities.

threat landscape – see **threatscape**.

threatscape – a term that amalgamates **threat** and land**scape**. An umbrella term to describe the overall, expected **method**s (**vectors**) and types of **cyber attackers** through or by which an organization or individual might expect to be **attack**ed.

three lines of defense – (UK: **three lines of defence**) – a security assurance model from the (now replaced) UK Financial Services Authority (FSA). The first tier describes the business (or operations level) and specifies who must own and be responsible for a company's information and **systems** and for following due process. The second tier describes the security management roles needed to provide the processes, **controls**, expertise and other framework elements that allow the business to operate within acceptable security **risk** tolerances. The final tier calls for **audit**ing those who verify that the first two tiers (lines of defense) are operating as they should.

TLD – acronym for **T**op-**L**evel **D**omain – the suffix part of a **domain**. For example, within cybersimplicity.*com*, it is the *.com* component that is considered to be the TLD. *.org, .gov* and *.info* are further examples of top level domains. See also **domain**.

TLS – see **Transport Layer Security**.

Top-Level Domain – see **TLD**.

TOR – is a free software **application** designed to protect the anonymity of the people who use it. The name is an acronym for 'The Onion Router,' the project from which the application evolved and a reference to how the software operates. Communications use multiple layers of **encryption** that enable them to travel through multiple locations without ever revealing both the originator and destination in any single step. At each step during the relay of the communication, only a single layer of the transmission route is revealed, with all remaining layers remaining encrypted. The final **IP address** destination is only revealed in the very last layer. The originating IP address of the communication is not revealed during any part of the communication relay, other than during the very first part of the relay. This mechanism is used to facilitate anonymous access to resources like the **darknet**.

traffic analysis – see **network traffic analysis**.

transmission control protocol (TCP) – the standard **method** used for **networks**, including the Internet, to send and receive error-free **data** that retains the same order that was originally intended.

transport layer security (TLS) – is a **cryptographic protocol**

(set of rules) for allowing secure communication between two digital locations. It is the successor to the Secure Socket Layer protocol, but is often referred to as being an **SSL** protocol. It is a form of **symmetrical encryption**.

triple DES – see **Data Encryption Standard**.

trojan – an **application** (**software program**) that appears to be harmless, but that actually hides and facilitates the operation of other, unseen malicious and unauthorized software programs and activities.

true negative – the correct recognition by a security technology or process of something that is harmless (not a security **threat**). See also **false positive, false negative** and **true positive**.

true positive – the correct recognition by a security technology or process of something that is a security **threat**. See also **false positive, false negative** and **true positive**.

trusted network – a group of interconnected **digital devices** in which the security **controls** and the assignment of **authorization**s and privileges are subject to a known and acceptable level of control. The opposite of an **untrusted network**.

two-factor authentication – see **multi-factor authentication**.

typosquatting – part of a **method** of **attack** in which the perpetrator acquires a **domain** name that looks at first glance to belong to a major organization. Attacks that leverage an incorrectly spelled domain are used in some forms of **phishing** and other **exploits**.

U is for URL

UEM – acronym for **U**nified **E**ndpoint **M**anagement. Technologies and processes that permit the diverse range of **digital devices** in use by any organization to have their **control** (management) simplified. The ability to apply common **policies** and standards to different user devices through a single **platform** or interface. A **method** of improving security **orchestration**.

unauthorized access – to gain entry without permission.

ungenious – something that was intended to achieve one goal but has a spectacularly negative outcome instead.

Unified Threat Management (**UTM**) – a type of security **device** or **application** that integrates a large number of security technologies and services. For example, a single **gateway** device that includes proxy **firewall**, **intrusion prevention**, gateway **anti-malware** and **VPN** functions.

untrusted network – a group of interconnected **digital devices** in which the security **controls** and/or assignment of **authorization**s and privileges are not subject to any centralized or acceptable level of control.

unvalidated redirects and forwards – one of the **OWASP** top 10 critical security flaws to guard against. If a **software program** sends a user or part of his or her information to a different website or webpage without adequately screening the destination, a **hacker** can hijack the unchecked routing instructions and redirect the user or misappropriate an instruction as part of a **cyber attack**.

URL – acronym for Uniform **R**esource **L**ocator. This is essentially the address (or path) where a particular destination can be found. For example, the main address for the Google website is the URL http://www.google.com

USB – acronym for **U**niversal **S**erial **B**us. This is a standard connector that exists on most computers, smartphones, tablets and other physical electronic **devices** that allow other electronic devices to be connected. Used for attaching a range of devices including keyboards, mice, external displays, printers and external storage devices.

US CERT – acronym for the **U**nited **S**tates **C**omputer **E**mergency **R**eadiness **T**eam.

user behavior analysis – to collate and review information about how the people who are using a specific **digital landscape** act. This helps determine behavior patterns and trends that can be used to design improved **cyber defense** and prevention measures.

user identity correlation – the collation and analysis of the **access rights** used by people within a specific group of authorized **system** users to understand their habits and behaviors. This information is used to validate these users' activities and to detect, and then prevent, unexpected, undesirable or **unauthorized access** usage. For example, user access **geo-location** can identify and block a user's log-in credentials from granting him or her access to a computer **network** if these credentials are used from two very distributed locations in an impossibly short period of time.

using components with known vulnerabilities – one of the **OWASP** top 10 critical security flaws to guard against. Most **applications** are built like construction kits and use many pre-fabricated parts. If any of the parts that are used are out of date or have active weaknesses (**exploits**) that can be exploited by criminals, this is considered to be a significant security issue. The building blocks used within software (known as the components) usually share the same permissions as the application they are part of. The use of any component that is compromised can allow an **attacker** to subvert the permissions of the software for use in a **cyber attack**. This flaw is likely to occur if the components used in an application are not checked and updated to address any known **vulnerabilities**. Due to the frequent use of large numbers of existing components in many software applications, this flaw is extremely common.

using known vulnerable components – . This term is a legacy OWASP top 10 security flaw that was replaced by the term **using components with known vulnerabilities**.

V is for Vector

vector – another word for '**method**,' as in 'They used multiple vectors for the **attack**.'

virtual desktop – a **virtual machine** that emulates the functions of a personal computer. See **virtual machine**.

virtual machine – a computer with an **operating system** that can run **applications** but that does not physically exist. Instead of running on an exclusive piece of physical hardware, the computer is merely a set of software and configuration files. Multiple virtual machines can exist on a single physical machine, or a single virtual machine can exist across multiple physical machines through the use of a **hypervisor**. Virtual machines are often used for security purposes, as they are quick to clean, easy to set up and useful for isolating **threats**.

virtual memory – a **method** of using hardware and software to create the impression of a larger active pool of computer thinking space than really exists. This can allow for more complex processes to run in machines with small memories at the cost of slowing down the speed of access to the information. The reduced speed is due to information being swapped between the real physical **memory** and the storage space (such as a hard disk) where the virtual information is being buffered.

virtual private network (VPN) – a **method** of providing a secure connection between two points over a public (or unsecure) infrastructure; for example, to set up a secure link between a remote company laptop in a hotel and the main company **network**.

virtual reality – a fully artificial, computer-generated simulation of a real environment. See also **augmented reality**.

virus – a form of **malware** that spreads by infecting (attaching itself to) other files and that usually seeks opportunities to continue this pattern. Viruses are now less common than other forms of malware, but were the main type of malware in very early computing. For that reason, people often refer to something as a virus when it is technically another form of malware.

vishing – abbreviation for **v**oice ph**ishing**. The use of a phone call or similar communication **method** (such as instant messaging) in which the caller attempts to deceive the recipient into performing an action (such as visiting a **URL**), or into revealing information that can then be used to obtain **unauthorized access** to **systems** or accounts. Usually, the ultimate purpose is to steal (or hold ransom) something of value. These types of calls are becoming extremely prevalent, as the criminal gangs involved may have already stolen part of the recipient's **data** (name, phone number...) to help persuade the person receiving the call that it is authentic and legitimate. As a rule, if you did not initiate a call or message, you should never comply with any demand, especially to visit any web page or link.

vulnerability – (in the context of **cybersecurity**) a weakness, usually in design, implementation or operation of software (including **operating systems**), that could be compromised and result in damage or harm.

vulnerability assessment – the identification and classification of security gaps in a computer, software **application**, **network** or other section of a **digital landscape**. This is usually a passive identification technique using **vulnerability scanning** that aims only to identify the gaps, without exploring how those gaps could be used in an **attack**. This should not be confused with a **penetration test**, which may include information from a vulnerability assessment, but which will go on to explore how any **vulnerabilities** can be **exploited**.

vulnerability scanning – the process of probing a **digital landscape**, usually through passive techniques, to determine any potential gaps or weaknesses in security. An example of a weakness can include software that is not running the latest version or **firewall port**s that should be secure but have been left open. This security technique may be used as part of a snapshot **vulnerability assessment** event or as part of a continuous security monitoring effort.

W is for White Hat

WannaCry – a notable malicious software (**malware**) **attack** launched in May 2017 that infected a large number of **devices** that were running out-of-date **operating system**s together with weak security configurations. This malware was notable because it leveraged a powerful (but known) **exploit** called **Eternal Blue**, along with a number of other exploits. Also noteworthy was the fact that this **cyber attack** highlighted how inadequate basic security measures were in a large number of enterprises. The malware itself also had substantial weaknesses; for instance, it had an embedded link cybersecurity detectives discovered could be used as a kill switch that stopped the malware from spreading. Experts eventually attributed this attack to a nation state. This event and a similar malware attack one month later (**NotPetya**) were regarded as a wake-up call for enterprises to improve their **compliance** with at least basic **cybersecurity** standards.

water holing – a **method** of **cyber attack** that identifies and infiltrates a location that a group of targets are known to visit frequently, for the purpose of infecting their **device**s with **malware**. Water holing can also be considered an example of the **social engineering** technique known as **baiting**.

web browser – the program a person uses on his or her **device** to view a web page. Examples of web browser programs include Internet Explorer and Firefox.

web server – is a computer that is used to host (provide) a web service or website.

wet wiring – creating connections between the human nervous system and **digital devices**. For example, sensors implanted in nerves in a **'smart'** prosthetic-user's body can transmit signals about the user's intent and position to a computer in the bionic prosthesis. The computer then translates the user's thoughts into actions performed by the **system** of motors, belts, and other components that allow the bionic limb to function very much like a natural limb.

white-box testing (also known as **clear-box testing**) – is the term used to describe a situation in which the technical layout (or source code) of the computer program being tested has been made available for the security test. This makes the test easier and cheaper to perform, but usually results in the identification of more issues than **black-box penetration testing** does. White-box testing can start early in the software lifecycle before an **application** has ever been installed in any production environments, making security fixes substantially cheaper and easier to apply.

white-hat – a security specialist who breaks into **systems** or **networks** by invitation (and with permission) from the owner, using only ethical means and with the intent to identify any security gaps that need to be addressed.

white-listing – the restriction of 'allowed' Internet sites or **data** packages to an explicit list of verified sources. For example, an organization operating a white-listed **firewall** can decide to only permit its **network** users to navigate to a restricted and verified list of Internet websites. This is the opposite of **black-listing**.

white team – the people who act as referees during any **ethical hacking** exercise conducted between a **red team** and a **blue team**.

wiper – a form of malicious software (**malware**) designed to delete the contents of a **digital device** to the extent that it can no longer be used without a full restoration of the original information from a **backup**.

Wireless Intrusion Prevention Systems (WIPS) – devices that can be attached to a **network** to check the radio spectrum for rogue or other **unauthorized access** points, and to then take countermeasures to help close down the **threat**.

worm – a form of malicious software (**malware**) that seeks to find other locations to which it can replicate. This helps to both protect the malware from removal and to increase the area of the **attack surface** that is compromised.

X is for XSS

XML EE – acronym for **XML E**xternal **E**ntities, also known as (XXE), is a new **OWASP** top 10 critical security flaw to guard against. XML is a language standard used across many **applications** and web services for communication. XML processing can be compromised in a significant number of ways. For example, by accepting an XML feed from a compromised external source, or through the use of any external reference that is compromised.

XSS – see **cross-site scripting**.

XSS hole – see **cross-site scripting**.

Y is for Y2K

Y2K – acronym representing the year 2000 technology **bug**. Organizations spent hundreds of millions of dollars before the year 2000 to ensure that their technologies were not taken out by the change of year in **systems** that were never designed to cope with a 4-digit year change. Before the year 2000, there was a very real fear that major catastrophes in the form of a technology meltdown could follow the date change. As the year change came and went with little to no impact, many organizations felt that they had been conned into excessive protective investments. Much of the resistance to adequate investments in **cybersecurity** can be attributed to the perceived over-investment in resolving this perceived technical issue.

Z is for Zero Day

zbot trojan – see **Zeus**.

zero-day – refers to the very first time a new type of **exploit** or new piece of **malware** is discovered. At that point in time, none of the **anti-virus, anti-malware** or other defenses may be set up to defend against the new form of exploit.

zero trust – an approach to deploying infrastructure and architecture securely that requires services and components to be verified and provided with **least privilege** before permitting any actions. This approach uses **micro-segmentation**, a form of **containerization** to keep components as discrete and separate as possible. Effectively, even the components within a network are not trusted by default. This method can be used to include cloud and other services outside of the **network** – to require that each service or other component is verified as trustworthy before use and even then only granted least privilege **access** to other components in the **digital landscape**.

Zeus – also known as **zbot**, is a form of **trojan malware** that can be used to target and steal confidential information (such as banking information) or to install **ransomware**. It has been around for some time (since 2007), but is subject to repeated improvements and variations. It continues to be one of the main forms of malware used in many **drive-by downloads** and **phishing attacks**. Once in place, it can operate by **keylogging**, **man-in-the-middle** attacks and other mechanisms.

zombie army – see **botnet**.

Numbers

0 day – see **zero-day** (**exploit**).

2FA – acronym for **two-factor authentication**. See **multi-factor authentication**.

3DES – see **Triple DES**.

3 lines of defense – see **three lines of defense**.

ABOUT THE BOOK AND AUTHOR

If you ever watched the British sitcom Blackadder II, specifically the episode on creating the first English dictionary – writing this book has been very much like that. New words are emerging all the time as the subject evolves.

If you have any new words you would like included in the next edition, please feel free to tweet the author (@RaefMeeuwisse) with the suggested word and any definition you are willing to allow the book to freely use as a starting point. The author avoided adding the 350 or so words that simply start with the word 'cyber'! The objective is to only include the most useful terms - and maybe some of the funnier ones.

Raef Meeuwisse is an active member of ISACA. He compiled and re-wrote the synchronized security and privacy control frameworks for two, multi-billion dollar companies. His experience also includes managing a global vendor technology audit service, designing a fully-integrated GRC platform, running massive global security programs, operating as a CISO and writing publications on cybersecurity. He enjoys speaking at very large conferences and at universities.

Made in the USA
Columbia, SC
21 February 2019